THE PRACTICAL NO GALLBLADDER DIET COOKBOOK

2200 Days of Mouthwatering Dishes Tailored for Gentle Digestion, Making Every Meal an Enjoyable Experience After Your Surgery

Cicely Vanwinkle

TABLE OF CONTENTS

CHAPTER 1: UNDERSTANDING YOUR NEW DIET

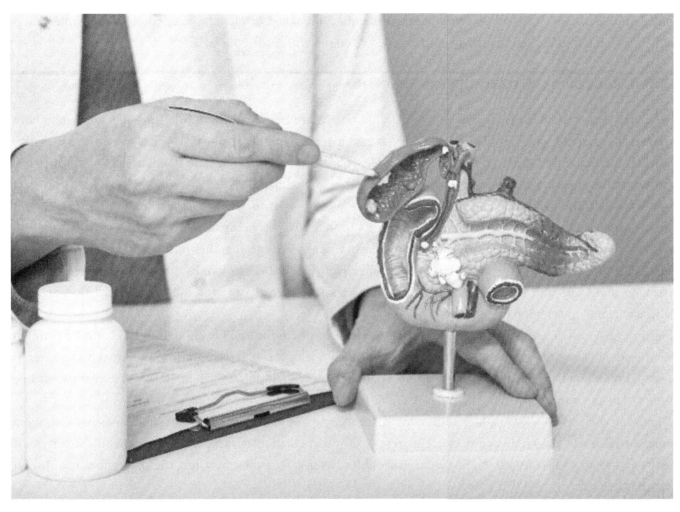

If you've recently had your gallbladder removed, you might be navigating what feels like a new realm in the world of eating and digestion. Surgical recovery not only mends our bodies but also necessitates adaptation, particularly when it comes to our diets. Embracing these changes can often be challenging yet can open doors to a much healthier and more pleasurable eating experience in your new digestive landscape.

The gallbladder, though small, played a crucial role in your body by storing bile, a fluid produced by the liver to help digest fats. Without it, the bile flows directly into the small intestine, which changes how your body handles food, especially fats. This might sound daunting, but with the correct guidance, you'll find that managing your diet becomes an intuitive part of your lifestyle.

You may experience some common digestive symptoms post-surgery such as bloating, diarrhea, or indigestion. While these symptoms are typical, managing them effectively can significantly improve your quality of life. This is where your knowledge about the right kinds of foods to eat (and those to avoid) becomes critical. Adjusting to your body's new normal means being mindful of what you eat and how it affects you.

Understanding your nutritional needs is another essential step. Without your gallbladder, eating large amounts of fatty food is a challenge for your system, so smaller, more frequent meals, which are easier to digest, might become a new norm for you. This doesn't imply a monotonous dietary routine but rather an opportunity to explore a wide array of foods that you can still enjoy. Variety in your diet ensures that you receive all the necessary nutrients to heal and maintain your body's balance.

As we move deeper into this journey together in "The Practical No Gallbladder Diet Cookbook", you'll discover not just the scientific 'whys' and 'hows' of your new diet, but also the practical and enjoyable ways through which you can adapt. Whether you're whipping up a quick breakfast or planning a celebratory meal, the goal is to help you make every bite gentle on your digestion and delightful for your palate.

1.1 THE ROLE OF THE GALLBLADDER IN DIGESTION

In the bustling city of our body, where organs and systems are perpetually at work, the gallbladder may have seemed like a small, quiet neighborhood café — not too prominent yet playing a vital role in the digestive process. Nestled under the liver, the gallbladder was your personal little assistant, handling fats with efficiency and precision, ensuring your digestive system didn't get overwhelmed.

Understanding the gallbladder begins with its basic function — storing and concentrating bile, a yellowish-brown digestive enzyme produced by the liver. Bile's primary duty is to break down fats into smaller droplets, which is crucial because fats are not water-soluble. They tend to clump together in the watery environment of our intestines, making it difficult for enzymes to effectively break them down. Bile acts as a sort of detergent, breaking these fats into tiny particles, thus providing a larger surface area for the pancreatic lipase, another crucial enzyme, to function effectively.

This interplay of bile and lipase ensures that fats are broken down thoroughly enough to be absorbed through the intestinal lining into the bloodstream. Here's a simpler analogy: if you were to drop oil into a dish of water, it would float in a big slick. Add a bit of dish soap, and you see that oil break apart. That's essentially what bile does to fats in your diet.

Whenever you ate, your gallbladder responded by squeezing out stored bile into the small intestine through a series of channels known as bile ducts. This response was meticulously timed to coincide with the arrival of fatty food from your stomach. Hence, your gallbladder ensured that there was just the right amount of bile at just the right time.

However, following the removal of your gallbladder — a surgical procedure known as a cholecystectomy — this precise orchestration changes. Now, bile from the liver drips continuously into the small intestine, but not necessarily in the larger, concentrated bursts that were once timed with meals. This can lead to a mismatch between the availability of bile and the presence of fats in the intestines, sparking some of the digestive discomforts many experience post-surgery.

The direct aftermath might include more frequent, looser stools or increased urgency to use the bathroom, particularly after eating fatty meals. This occurs because without the gallbladder's reservoir capacity, the bile that trickles in may not be sufficient to adequately handle a large influx of fat at once. In response, unprocessed fats pass through the digestive tract and can cause diarrhea, a phenomenon known as bile acid diarrhea or bile acid malabsorption.

Moreover, adjustments in bile management can also affect the absorption of fat-soluble vitamins like A, D, E, and K. These vitamins depend heavily on adequate bile for their absorption into the body. With fluctuating bile levels, your body might not absorb these essential nutrients as efficiently as before.

Despite these challenges, the human body is remarkably adaptable. Over time, several adaptations occur. The liver can somewhat adjust the amount of bile it produces, and the bile ducts may increase in size to hold more bile, partially compensating for the absence of the gallbladder. While these adjustments help, they often require supportive dietary strategies to function smoothly.

This transition necessitates a period of dietary reevaluation and adjustment. Smaller, more frequent meals can prevent the overload of fats that your system is less equipped to handle all at once. Emphasizing foods lower in fat and higher in fiber can also help regulate the passage of food through your intestines, providing a more even, manageable workflow for bile. It is also beneficial to maintain a level of mindfulness towards how different foods affect your body in this new digestive environment.

Understanding the role of your gallbladder in digestion sets the stage for adapting to life without it. While the initial adjustment phase might be accompanied by discomfort and trial-and-error with foods, gaining knowledge about these processes provides a foundation for smoother adaptation. With time and thoughtful dietary adjustments, you can continue to enjoy a fulfilling and nutritionally sound diet that supports your health and keeps symptoms at bay. Remember, without your gallbladder, your digestive system functions differently, not necessarily less effectively. With the right strategies, you can still lead a healthy, active life post-surgery. Indeed, this change can be a compelling invitation to get better acquainted with your body's needs and how best to support them through nutrition.

1.2 COMMON SYMPTOMS AFTER GALLBLADDER REMOVAL

Life after gallbladder removal, or cholecystectomy, can feel like navigating a new terrain with familiar landmarks strangely altered. The gallbladder might be a small organ, but its impact on digestion is significant, and its removal brings about a variety of symptoms that manifest as your body adapts to a new way of processing food. For many, understanding and managing these symptoms is a pivotal step towards regaining a comfortable and healthful life.

One of the most immediate changes you may notice is an alteration in bowel patterns. The absence of the gallbladder leads to a continuous drip of bile into the intestines, rather than controlled releases. This can result in more urgent and frequent trips to the bathroom, particularly after meals rich in fats. Known as bile acid diarrhea, this condition occurs because excess bile in the intestine can act as a laxative.

Another common complaint post-surgery is bloating and gas, which often accompany a feeling of fullness. Without the gallbladder to regulate the flow of bile, fat digestion becomes less efficient. Gases produced by the fermentation of undigested foods can accumulate, causing discomfort and bloating.

Heartburn and indigestion are also frequent concerns. These can be attributed to changes in the way food moves through your digestive system and how bile interacts with stomach acids. Bile reflux, a condition where bile flows into the stomach, can exacerbate these sensations, leading to discomfort.

While less common, some people may experience nausea or even vomiting. These symptoms can be particularly prevalent in the immediate weeks following surgery as the body adapts to the changes. Over time, these symptoms may decrease in intensity and frequency as the digestive system adjusts to its new normal.

Additionally, adjustments in fat absorption can affect your overall nutrition. The gallbladder's role in emulsifying fats means it was central in facilitating the absorption of fat-soluble vitamins such as Vitamins A, D, E, and K. After its removal, you might find it challenging to absorb these essential nutrients efficiently, possibly leading to deficiencies if dietary adaptations are not made.

Weight fluctuations can also occur. Some individuals might lose weight due to a reduction in fat absorption, while others may gain weight as they adjust their diet to include more carbohydrates and less fat to mitigate digestive discomfort.

It's important to note that pain, although less commonly discussed, can also continue post-surgery. This might be due to several factors, including the formation of scar tissue, continuing issues with bile ducts, or other underlying conditions that were not resolved with the removal of the gallbladder.

Taking control of these symptoms often begins with a keen observation of how your body reacts to different foods and conditions. Small, frequent meals can help manage the workload on your digestive system, reducing symptoms such as diarrhea and bloating. Choosing low-fat options and increasing dietary fiber can aid in normalizing bowel movements and enhancing overall digestive comfort.

Staying hydrated is another crucial element. Increased fluid intake can help manage diarrhea and support overall digestive health. Furthermore, introducing probiotics, either through diet or supplements, can help balance intestinal flora, which, in turn, can alleviate gas and bloating.

Managing fat intake does not mean eliminating fats entirely — healthy fats are an essential part of digestion and overall health. Instead, incorporating small amounts of healthy fats gradually and monitoring how your body reacts can help you find a balance that suits your new digestive capabilities.

For those experiencing continual discomfort or unexpected symptoms like severe pain or jaundice, consulting with a healthcare provider is essential. Sometimes, symptoms might indicate other conditions such as bile duct injuries or stones, which require professional attention.

Understanding, anticipating, and managing these common symptoms are keys to adjusting to life without a gallbladder. While the journey may involve some trial and error, it is also an opportunity to develop a deeper understanding of your body's needs and responses. By arming yourself with knowledge and supported by dietary strategies, you can navigate this new landscape effectively, finding not only relief but also a renewed sense of well-being.

1.3 NUTRITIONAL NEEDS WITHOUT A GALLBLADDER

Navigating the nutritional landscape without a gallbladder involves a thoughtful balance, a willingness to adapt, and an understanding of the essential nutrients your body now processes differently. This journey is not just about subtraction — removing certain foods or fats — but also about recalibrating and enriching your diet to foster optimal digestion and nutrient absorption.

In the absence of your gallbladder, your liver continues to produce bile, but without a storage unit, bile is continuously released into your intestines, albeit in smaller quantities. This changes how your body handles fats and consequently, fat-soluble vitamins (A, D, E, and K). Ensuring you receive adequate amounts of these, along with other critical nutrients, is paramount for maintaining health and vitality post-surgery.

Optimizing Fat Intake

The relationship between fats and your body post-cholecystectomy is nuanced. While it's wise to moderate fat intake to avoid digestive upset, fats are still essential. They're vital for energy, cell growth, protecting your organs, and facilitating the absorption of vitamins. The key is to focus on easily digestible fats. Omega-3 fatty acids, found in fish like salmon and in flaxseeds, are highly beneficial. They assist in reducing inflammation and are generally easier on digestion compared to saturated fats found in high-fat meats and full-fat dairy products.

Moreover, incorporating medium-chain triglycerides (MCTs), found in foods like coconut oil, might be easier for you to digest. Unlike long-chain fatty acids, MCTs travel straight to the liver where they are quickly used for energy, less likely to stir bile-related issues.

Linoleum Lapses and Vitamin Vitality

Vitamin deficiencies can occur post-gallbladder surgery, particularly concerning fat-soluble vitamins (A, D, E, K). Vitamin D and calcium are crucial for bone health, Vitamin A for eyesight and skin, Vitamin E for its antioxidant properties, and Vitamin K for blood clotting. To manage this, a diet rich in lean proteins, vegetables, fruits, and whole grains is beneficial. Foods like sweet potatoes, carrots, spinach, and dairy products can boost vitamin A; fortified cereals and fatty fish can enhance vitamin D levels.

For vitamin E, consider incorporating nuts and seeds, while leafy greens can bolster your Vitamin K intake. In some cases, a supplement might be necessary, but it's wise to consult with a healthcare provider to tailor these additions to your distinct needs.

Fiber: Your Digestive Friend

Fiber plays an indispensable role, especially without a gallbladder. Soluble fiber, found in foods like oats, fruits, and legumes, helps absorb excess bile and improve bowel movements. Insoluble fiber from vegetables, wheat bran, and whole grains promotes healthy digestion and adds bulk to stool, mitigating the risk of diarrhea — a common post-operative complaint. Including a balance of both types of fiber can support the digestive process and provide a feeling of fullness, which can prevent overeating.

Mindful Meal Management

Small, frequent meals can prevent the small intestine from being overwhelmed by fats and can reduce symptoms like bloating and diarrhea. This meal strategy diminishes the demand placed on bile and eases the digestion process. Each meal should be well-rounded and nutrient-dense to support overall health and ensure adequate intake of essential nutrients.

Hydration: A Simple yet Powerful Tool

Increasing fluid intake is crucial. Water does more than just quench thirst; it facilitates the transport of nutrients and the elimination of waste. It also helps manage bile consistency and supports overall digestive functions. Ensuring a good intake of fluids throughout the day can significantly aid with digestion and alleviate some symptoms associated with gallbladder removal.

A Note on Probiotics

The introduction of probiotics into the diet can also be beneficial. These beneficial bacteria can help balance your gut flora, which may be disrupted post-surgery. Foods rich in probiotics such as yogurt, kefir, and fermented vegetables, or a quality probiotic supplement, can aid in digestion and help maintain an intestinal environment that supports nutrient absorption and immune function.

Understanding your body's new needs and responses after gallbladder removal is an ongoing process. It's akin to recalibrating a complex and sensitive system. Your diet plays a pivotal role in this recalibration, helping smooth the transition and mitigate symptoms. Armed with knowledge and guided by experience, adapting your dining habits in this new phase of life not only makes you a manager of your digestion but a curator of your overall well-being.

As you embark on this journey, remember the adaptability of the human body is vast, and with gradual dietary tweaks and mindful eating, you can lead a healthful, vibrant life, even without a gallbladder. This nutritional voyage, while challenging, invites curiosity and offers a pathway to deeper understanding of your body's intricate workings and needs.

CHAPTER 2: ESSENTIAL ALIMENTARY TIPS

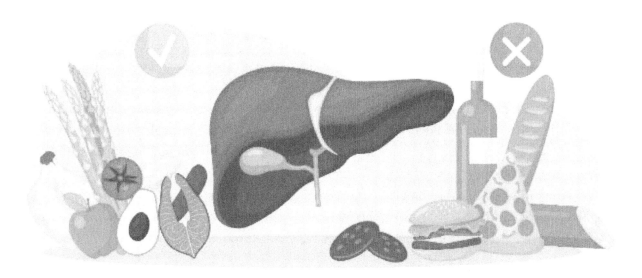

Embarking on a gastronomic journey post-gallbladder surgery can feel like navigating a maze without a map. As you've learned in the previous chapter about the pivotal functions your gallbladder used to play, you might now be pondering the implications of its absence and how to adapt without discomfort. Here in Chapter 2, "Essential Alimentary Tips," we delve into the nitty-gritty: which foods will become your allies, as well as those you might consider leaving behind.

Imagine you're at a farmers' market: there are rows upon rows of vibrant produce, grains, and proteins. Some of these will nourish and energize you without a second thought, while others require more caution. Let's take this stroll through the market together, shall we? I'll guide you to embrace the foods you need, showcasing how they benefit your new dietary framework.

Let's talk about fats—or more precisely, the types that your body can now handle better. While the full, rich flavor of a slab of buttered toast might once have been your morning ritual, lighter alternatives like avocado or olive oil can become your new favorites. Consider these healthy fats not just as substitutions, but as delicious opportunities to reinvent your dishes in ways you might never have explored otherwise.

it's important to consider not just what you eat, but how much. The art of portion control is less about restriction and more about balance. Just as a chef knows that the right amount of seasoning can make or break a dish, the proper portion sizes can be crucial to ensuring that your meals are satisfying yet gentle on your digestive system. Navigating these changes isn't just about following a set of rules—it's about listening to your body, adapting with care, and occasionally indulging in your culinary creativity. By the end of this chapter, I hope you feel equipped, not just with knowledge, but with the confidence to tailor your diet in ways that bring joy and comfort back to your table. Let's keep walking this path together, exploring and adjusting. With every meal, you're not just feeding your body; you're nurturing your resilience and reclaiming your zest for life.

2.1 FOODS TO AVOID

In the broad tapestry of post-surgery life, understanding what foods might need to be tucked away, at least for a while, can feel somewhat daunting. You're not merely navigating a diet; you're recalibrating how your body processes every bite. Without your gallbladder as a partner, certain foods can disrupt rather than nourish.

Imagine you're recalibrating a beloved old clock. It still tells time, but it needs a gentler touch and more delicate tuning. Your diet is somewhat similar—what used to be suitable may now necessitate caution or even avoidance. Let's start with **fatty foods**. This is about more than just skipping that extra dollop of cream or selecting leaner cuts of meat. Your gallbladder once managed fat digestion by storing bile and releasing it judiciously. Without this storage unit, bile drips continuously into the intestine but in smaller amounts, insufficient for breaking down large amounts of fat. Thus, heavy, greasy foods like deep-fried treats or fatty cuts of meat can become provocateurs of discomfort, leading to bloating and pain.

Fast food is often crafted with convenience rather than wellness in mind; high in calories and low in nutritional value, these meals also tend to be laden with fats that your body will now struggle to process. Picture your digestive system as a newly assigned orchestra conductor who has yet to master guiding the ensemble through complex symphonies of fats and oils—they need simpler sheet music, at least initially.

Moving onto **spicy foods**, while they tantalize the taste buds, they can also stimulate the stomach to produce more acid. For someone without a gallbladder, this increase in gastric acid can lead to discomfort and heartburn. It's similar to turning up the heat in a sensitive greenhouse; it's all too easy to cross the line from balmy to overwhelming.

Conversations around **highly processed foods** also come into play. These items are often high in refined sugars and artificial additives, which can exacerbate symptoms of indigestion and bloating. Imagine filling a finely-tuned engine with low-grade oil; it's likely to sputter and stall instead of running smoothly.

However, let's not forget **dairy products**. Rich, high-fat dairy products can be particularly challenging. Cheese, ice cream, and full-fat milk can cause your system to labor more intensely, attempting to break down more fat with less bile. It's like asking someone to clean a large house with just a small broom; the task is possible but far from efficient.

We should also carefully consider **legumes**. Though nutritionally dense and generally part of a healthy diet, beans and lentils can cause gaseous discomfort and bloating for those without a gallbladder. The reason? Your digestive system is now more sensitive to legumes' complex sugars which can ferment in the gut. It's akin to attending a bustling party when you're seeking quiet — the environment is no longer as compatible as it once was.

Cruciferous vegetables such as broccoli, cauliflower, and cabbage, while packed with nutrients and beneficial fibers, can similarly lead to gas build-up. This isn't to say they must be avoided entirely, but they should be introduced slowly and in small portions to assess tolerance. It's about learning how much your 'digestive audience' can handle before the theater gets too loud.

Moreover, **sweets and sugary beverages** deserve caution. Not only do they offer little nutrition, but their rapid digestion can also lead to quick, intense energy spikes followed by equally swift drops — a rollercoaster that can stress your already sensitive system.

Lastly, there are **nutritive sweeteners like high fructose corn syrup**, often hidden in processed foods and drinks. These can pull fluid into the intestine, leading to diarrhea, a particularly unwelcome guest in your new dietary life.

Navigating this new terrain isn't about deprivation — think of it more as becoming a discerning gourmet who selects only the finest, most agreeable ingredients. Each individual is different; what might cause discomfort in one person can be perfectly fine in another. Hence, it is crucial to listen to your body and notice how different foods affect you, potentially adjusting your diet along the way.

As we wrap up this discussion on foods to avoid or limit intake of, consider how gradual adjustments rather than drastic eliminations can enhance your quality of life. Introduce changes slowly, monitor how you feel, and build your diet around foods that support and nourish without causing distress. This careful tuning and retuning of your dietary demands aren't just about avoiding pain or discomfort; it's about crafting a life brimming with joy and good health.

In the next pages, we will explore the foods to embrace, those that will not only be gentle on your system but also contribute to a fulfilling and healthful dietary journey, ensuring each meal brings you comfort and delight.

2.2 FOODS TO EMBRACE

Transitioning to a diet without the support of your gallbladder is much like learning to dance with a new partner. It requires understanding, patience, and a bit of practice. While we've discussed foods best sidestepped in this new dance, it's equally crucial to highlight those which glide smoothly with you on this journey: Foods to embrace that not only nourish but also delight without causing distress.

Low-fat dairy alternatives top our list of favorable options. Think of almond milk, low-fat yogurt, and cottage cheese. These foods provide the comfort and calcium of dairy without the high fat content that can overwhelm your system. Imagine them as graceful dancers in the ballet of your digestion, light on their feet and easy to partner with.

Lean proteins are your next companions. Lean cuts of chicken, turkey, fish, and even plant-based proteins like tofu stand in contrast to their fatty relatives by being easier to digest. They provide the essential amino acids necessary for tissue repair and muscle growth without the extra burden of fat digestion. Engage with these proteins as you would a trusted friend who supports without overwhelming.

Grains, especially whole grains, play a pivotal role. Foods like brown rice, quinoa, and whole grain breads offer a source of energy that is released slowly, providing a steady source of fuel without causing spikes in blood sugar. Include them in your meals as the solid foundation of your culinary creations; they're dependable and sustaining, much like the bass notes in a well-composed song.

Fruits and vegetables, particularly those that are less likely to cause bloating, should become staples. Carrots, bell peppers, spinach, and ripe bananas are not only colorful and packed with vitamins, but they're also kind to your digestive tract. Envision preparing a vibrant palette of paint for your next masterpiece – these fruits and veggies add color and life to your plate and body.

Healthy fats should not be forgotten. While you need to lower your fat intake overall, fats from sources like avocados, nuts, seeds, and olive oil are crucial for absorbing fat-soluble vitamins and providing energy. Such fats are akin to a gentle drizzle of oil on an intricate machine, ensuring everything runs smoothly without clogging up the works.

What about flavor enhancers? Fresh herbs and spices not only add flavor without the negative impact of heavy sauces or seasonings, but many, like turmeric and ginger, offer anti-inflammatory benefits. Picture these as the exotic spices traded along the Silk Road, each carrying their unique story and zest that can transform simple dishes into aromatic feasts without aggravating your system.

Hydration plays an underrated yet critical role. Hydration doesn't just come from water – broth, herbal teas, and water-rich fruits like watermelon contribute to maintaining fluid balance in your body. Think of water as the music setting the rhythm for your digestive system's dance, essential and ever-present.

Including fermented foods like kefir, yogurt, and sauerkraut can be a boon, as they contain probiotics that aid digestion and help maintain gut health. Introducing them into your diet is akin to starting a new hobby that benefits your wellbeing, gradually building a better rhythm in your digestive process.

Lastly, let us not overlook the importance of portion size and food preparation. Gentle cooking methods like steaming, boiling, grilling, or baking can make foods easier to digest. Improper portion sizes, however, can be as disruptive as a misstep in tango. It's not just what you eat; it's how much and how it's prepared.

Remember, crafting a new diet is a process that requires tweaking and personalization. Start with these supportive food choices and monitor how you feel. Adjust as necessary, and don't rush the process. Your body will begin to harmonize with these foods, leading to improved health and comfort.

As we conclude this section, picture yourself mastering the art of your new diet. Each meal is an opportunity to nourish and care for your body, ensuring every bite is a step towards better health. Embrace these foods wholeheartedly, as each plays a critical role in your journey to recovery and comfort.

2.3 MANAGING PORTION SIZES

Once you've acquainted yourself with the right kinds of foods to incorporate into your post-gallbladder removal diet, the next vital step is mastering how much to eat at any given time. The concept of portion size management is crucial, particularly after surgery, when your body's ability to digest large amounts of food at once can be significantly compromised. Think of this shift not just as reducing the quantity of what you eat, but rather as refining the calibration of your meals to suit your new digestive framework.

Consider the effect of a massive feast on a small, delicate dinner plate. It's overwhelming, isn't it? The same can be said of your digestive system post-surgery. Without your gallbladder's bile storage capabilities, consuming large portions at once can lead to discomfort such as bloating, diarrhea, and indigestion. It's much like expecting a small backpack to hold the contents of a large suitcase. The strategy, therefore, lies in scaling down the load to better accommodate your digestive tract's new capacity.

The journey begins with understanding the size of a healthy portion. For many, the default setting at mealtime is to fill the plate, often leading to unintentional overeating. However, your new dietary lifestyle beckons for a shift towards mindful eating—where the focus is on the quality of your food and the appropriateness of your portions more than just the sheer quantity.

A simple yet effective approach to manage portion sizes is to use smaller plates. By doing so, the same amount of food appears more filling when served on a smaller dish as opposed to being lost on a large plate. This visual trick helps signal to your brain that you're consuming a full plate's worth, aiding in satisfaction even though the actual quantity is reduced.

Besides choosing smaller dishware, the method of "hand measuring" can be quite effective. For proteins, a portion roughly the size of your palm provides an individualized measure, tailored to your body's size. Carbohydrates, ideally, should fit into your cupped hand, while fat portions—like a dollop of olive oil or a slice of avocado—should be about the size of your thumb.

Mindful eating practices further enhance portion control. It involves paying full attention to the experience of eating and drinking, both inside and outside the body. Watch for cues that your hunger is satisfied, which typically can take up to twenty minutes to register. Eating slowly not only allows you to truly savor the flavors but also helps prevent overeating by giving your body the time it needs to acknowledge fullness.

However, it's not all about self-restriction. Managing portion sizes also includes understanding how often you should eat. Small, frequent meals can keep hunger at bay while preventing the overload of your digestive system. Aim for evenly spaced meals throughout the day, perhaps five to six small meals, rather than three large ones. This keeps your energy levels steady and your metabolism active, making digestion easier.

Meal planning also plays an integral role in managing food quantities effectively. By planning your meals in advance, you're more likely to prepare portions that are just right for your needs, thereby avoiding the temptation to eat directly from a larger container—which can lead to eating more than intended. Consider using portion-controlled containers for storing and carrying meals, which takes the guesswork out of serving sizes and is particularly useful for those with busy lifestyles.

Despite these tips and strategies, remember that dietary adjustments post-gallbladder removal are highly personal. What works for one may not work for another. It's beneficial to maintain a food diary initially, logging not just what and how much you eat, but also any reactions you have to different foods and portion sizes. This diary can be a critical tool in understanding your body's responses and tailoring further dietary adjustments accordingly.

Finally, embrace flexibility in your approach. Some days your body may handle a certain food in a small quantity perfectly well, while on others, it may not. Listen attentively to its signals and be prepared to adjust your portion sizes as necessary. This process is not about strict limitations or rigorous dietary constraints but about finding a balance that makes you feel your best while ensuring your nutritional needs are met.

CHAPTER 3: BALANCING YOUR DIET

Finding balance—it's a concept as essential to our diets as it is to our everyday lives, especially in the context of your journey after gallbladder surgery. Imagine your diet as a beautifully orchestrated symphony; each instrument, or food group, must harmonize, neither too overpowering nor too faint, to create a melody that soothes and energizes the body. This chapter aims to guide you through setting this symphonic balance in your meals, ensuring every nutrient plays its part beautifully, tailored to the needs of a body adapting to life without a gallbladder.

Introducing healthy fats into your diet can seem counterintuitive after your surgery, with common misunderstandings suggesting a near-total fat elimination. However, the reality is more nuanced and far from a fat-free regime. Think of healthy fats like olive oil or avocados as the string section of our orchestra—essential, rounding out the melody, enhancing the dish's flavors while absorbing important fat-soluble vitamins.

Next, let's consider protein—the brass section of our dietary symphony. It's robust, vital, and needs to be approached with a sense of moderation and selection. Lean meats, fish, and plant-based proteins can support your digestion and sustain muscle without overwhelming your system.

And we cannot overlook the role of fiber—our woodwinds, if you will—offering a gentle yet powerful component that helps regulate digestion and maintain satiety. Fibrous foods like fruits, vegetables, and whole grains, when introduced gradually and consistently, can significantly improve how you process meals and reduce post-meal discomforts.

Balancing these elements does not require perfection but rather a continual adjustment, much like tuning instruments before a performance, to find what best suits your unique composition. Through strategic choices and informed combinations, this chapter strives not only to minimize discomfort but also to reinstate joy and satisfaction in every meal, making the art of eating well a source of daily delight and comfort.

3.1 INCORPORATING HEALTHY FATS

In the wake of gallbladder surgery, adjusting your diet to meet your body's altered processing capabilities is paramount, and perhaps no component requires more attentive rebalancing than fats. The removal of your gallbladder doesn't end the narrative of fats in your diet; rather, it introduces a new chapter, one where these vital players need to be carefully orchestrated to ensure they contribute positively to your digestion and overall health.

Healthy fats are not merely a part of your diet; they are crucial enablers of healing and daily function. They assist in the absorption of vitamins A, D, E, and K and are essential for hormonal balance and cellular health. However, without the gallbladder's reservoir of bile on hand to aid fat digestion, the body must adapt to digesting fats with the limited, continuous flow of bile directly from the liver.

This adaptation calls for a strategic approach to incorporating fats: selecting the right types and managing the amounts. The fats to focus on are primarily unsaturated fats, found in plants and fish, which have been shown to support heart health and reduce inflammation—two factors particularly crucial in post-surgical recovery. These beneficial fats come in two main forms: monounsaturated and polyunsaturated fats.

Monounsaturated fats, found in olive oil, avocados, and certain nuts, play a melody that keeps your heart rhythmically healthy and your cholesterol levels in check. The gentle nature of these fats makes them ideal for your modified digestion system. Imagine drizzling a rich, golden olive oil over a salad or mashing a ripe avocado for a soothing, creamy spread on whole-grain toast; these are not only culinary delights but also friends to your recuperating body.

Polyunsaturated fats, including omega-3 and omega-6 fatty acids, offer their own spectrum of benefits. Omega-3 acids, especially evident in fatty fish like salmon, sardines, and mackerel, act as powerful anti-inflammatory agents. They are akin to a soothing balm that calms internal inflammations, potentially aiding the healing post-surgery tissues. Then there are the omega-6 fatty acids, found in certain oils like safflower and sunflower. While necessary, these should be consumed in moderation, as the Western diet tends to heavily skew towards omega-6 fats, which, in excessive amounts, can tip the scales towards inflammation.

Integrating these fats into your diet doesn't call for grand upheavals but rather thoughtfully planned modifications. The aim is to provide your liver with manageable amounts of fats that it can process in its steady, albeit less efficient, drip of bile. This could mean opting for a piece of steamed salmon seasoned with herbs rather than a pan-fried steak. It involves choosing dressings made with walnut oil or flaxseed oil, which not only add flavor but a boost of omega-3 to your meals, aiding both your salads and your cellular structures.

Moreover, the strategic use of cooking methods can greatly enhance your body's ability to handle these healthier fats. Steaming, baking, or poaching can be more beneficial compared to frying, as these methods do not overwhelm the digestive process. When sautéing, it's prudent to use just enough oil to coat the pan, or perhaps employ a non-stick spray to minimize the amount of fat needed.

A key to successfully incorporating fats into a no-gallbladder diet also lies in the frequency and quantity of fat intake. Small, regular amounts of fat are preferable over large amounts consumed infrequently. This approach helps ensure a consistent, manageable flow of fats through your liver and intestines, reducing the likelihood of digestive upset. Regular but moderate consumption of healthy fats also aids in maintaining your energy levels and supports a feeling of satiety after meals, which can help in managing portion sizes and preventing weight gain.

Beyond the types and amounts of fats, the context in which they are consumed can also impact how well they are digested. Pairing fats with high-fiber foods, for example, can help to regulate the speed of digestion, ensuring that fats are more gradually absorbed and less likely to cause distress. A slice of avocado on a whole-grain toast is a classic pairing that marries healthy fats with fiber for a satisfying, digestion-friendly meal option.

Understanding and adjusting to your body's new way of handling fats post-gallbladder removal does not have to be a daunting task. With the right information, thoughtful planning, and a dash of culinary creativity, fats can continue to play a supportive and enjoyable role in your diet. Rather than seeing the absence of your gallbladder as a limitation, it can be a valuable opportunity to get intimately acquainted with your dietary needs, learning how to nourish yourself delicately and efficiently in this new phase of life. Indeed, every meal can become a harmonious concert of flavors and nutrients that not only tastes delightful but also fundamentally supports your ongoing health and well-being.

3.2 PROTEIN SOURCES AND DIGESTION

Navigating the realm of protein intake after gallbladder removal can feel somewhat akin to rediscovering your culinary rhythm. Proteins, essential to healing and everyday vitality, must be approached with a nuanced understanding of your body's altered digestion process. Consider proteins as the robust pillars of your diet that must be well-suited to a landscape that now lacks the gallbladder's aid in digestion.

The gallbladder played a crucial role in digesting fats, which indirectly supported the digestion of proteins by emulsifying fats that could otherwise hinder protein breakdown. Without this support, your body faces a greater challenge in processing high-fat protein sources, which makes the choice and preparation of proteins more critical than ever.

Lean proteins are the superheroes in the post-gallbladder diet. They are easier for your body to handle and reduce the likelihood of digestive discomfort. Foods such as chicken breast, turkey, lean cuts of pork, and fish not only provide essential amino acids required for rebuilding tissues and supporting immune function but also ensure that your digestive system is not unduly burdened.

Fish, particularly those rich in omega-3 fatty acids like salmon, mackerel, and sardines, offer double benefits. They contribute to your protein intake while also providing an anti-inflammatory effect, which can be particularly beneficial during the healing process and beyond. The low-fat content in these fish makes them an ideal choice, as they are digestible and heart-healthy.

Plant-based proteins, including lentils, chickpeas, and quinoa, are crucial not only because of their protein content but also because they bring a wealth of fiber into the diet. This fiber can act buffer, regulating the digestion speed and ensuring a smoother digestive process. Incorporating a variety of plant-based proteins can also prevent common post-surgical issues like constipation and maintain the health of your gut microbiome.

Another vital aspect of adapting your protein consumption is the consideration of how proteins are prepared. Cooking methods that require less oil and fat, such as grilling, steaming, or baking, are preferable. Techniques involving heavy creams, sauces, or deep-frying are best minimized or adjusted to accommodate your new dietary needs.

It's not just the type of protein and cooking method that matters, but also how it is eaten. Consuming smaller, more frequent protein portions can alleviate the workload on your digestive system, allowing it more time and energy to efficiently process each meal. This pacing not only helps in digestion but could also enhance the absorption of nutrients, stabilizing energy levels throughout the day.

However, it's also wise to consider the symbiotic relationships between proteins and other nutrients. For instance, combining protein with non-starchy vegetables can aid in digestion and nutrient uptake. Vegetables not only provide fiber, which helps in moving food smoothly through the digestive tract, but their alkaline nature can also balance the acids needed to break down protein, ensuring a more even digestion process.

On the flip side, it's crucial to be intuitive with your body's signals. Not every recommended food will be right for every individual. It's possible that what works well for one person may cause discomfort for another. Paying close attention to how your body reacts to different types of proteins, and adjusting accordingly, is a critical practice. Keeping a food diary can be an incredibly effective tool in tracking which proteins—and in what combinations—serve you best.

Moreover, as you continue to adjust to life without a gallbladder, remember that the journey is not just about adapting to a new way of eating but rediscovering the joy and nourishment in meals. Protein, with its vital role in your diet, can be both a source of comfort and a path to exploration. From the sizzle of a well-cooked piece of lean steak to the comforting warmth of a lentil soup, each meal is an opportunity to nurture not just your body but also your spirit.

Ultimately, the path to effective protein digestion and utilization in a no-gallbladder diet lies in the thoughtful selection, preparation, and timing of protein consumption. By managing these aspects, you can support your body's healing, maintain your energy levels, and continue to enjoy the pleasures of eating well.

3.3 IMPORTANCE OF FIBER

Fiber often doesn't receive the limelight it deserves, especially when discussing diets following gallbladder removal. Yet, understanding its role and effectively integrating it into your diet could make a substantial difference in managing your digestive health and overall well-being. Think of fiber as the conductor of the orchestra that is your digestive system, guiding the food smoothly through the digestive tract and aiding the body's natural rhythm of absorption and elimination.

Without your gallbladder, the digestion process changes. Your liver continues to produce bile, but it drips continuously into the intestine rather than being stored and concentrated in the gallbladder. As such, digestion becomes a more constant process, requiring a balanced, thoughtful intake of food—here, fiber plays a pivotal role.

Imagine fiber as a gentle guide that helps pace the digestion process, making it more manageable for your body to absorb nutrients and process fats with the available bile. Soluble fiber, found in oats, apples, carrots, and flaxseeds, turns into a gel-like substance when mixed with water. This gel binds with fatty substances in the intestines, including bile acids, which can help manage cholesterol levels by removing them from the body as waste. More importantly, this binding helps to regulate the digestion of fats, which is critical without the gallbladder to regulate bile release.

Insoluble fiber, on the other hand, acts more like a broom, sweeping through your digestive tract and aiding bowel health. Found in foods like whole grains, nuts, and many vegetables, insolubility fiber does not dissolve in water, which helps add bulk to the stool and ensures that waste moves through your digestive system efficiently and regularly. This can help prevent the constipation that sometimes accompanies the changes in your digestive process post-surgery.

Introducing fiber into one's diet post-gallbladder removal must be a gradual process. A sudden increase can lead to uncomfortable bloating and gas because your gut needs time to adjust to digesting increased amounts of fiber. Starting with smaller amounts and progressively increasing the intake allows your body to adapt without discomfort.

Pairing fiber with adequate hydration is equally essential. The water helps dissolve soluble fiber, which facilitates its smooth passage and function within the digestive system. Moreover, water helps push insoluble fiber through the digestive tract, preventing blockages and easing the movement of waste.

But beyond just aiding digestion, fiber provides several long-term health benefits. It helps regulate blood sugar levels by slowing down glucose absorption into the bloodstream, which can prevent spikes in blood sugar and insulin levels. For those who have undergone gallbladder removal, maintaining a balanced blood sugar level can significantly impact energy levels and overall health.

Moreover, a diet rich in high-fiber foods can contribute to heart health. The reduction of bile acids through fiber's binding properties helps to pull cholesterol from the heart, aiding in the prevention of heart disease. Additionally, fiber's role in weight control is vital, as it aids in satiety and helps prevent overeating, a crucial factor in maintaining a healthy weight post-surgery.

The integration of fiber into each meal requires mindfulness. It begins with understanding the sources of both soluble and insoluble fiber and knowing how much of each to introduce into your diet. Encouraging a variety of fiber sources can not only enhance the nutritional profile but also keeps meals interesting. From the crunch of a raw carrot to the comforting warmth of oatmeal, these textures and tastes contribute to meal satisfaction.

To truly benefit from fiber's dietary support, one must also consider the timing of intake. Distributing fiber consumption throughout the day can prevent the overload at any one time, supporting steady digestion and providing consistent energy levels.

Educating yourself about the types of fiber and their benefits can lead to more informed food choices, turning meal planning into a proactive tool for managing your health. Fiber doesn't just support the digestive system; it enhances overall vitality and well-being, making it a cornerstone of your diet in your post-gallbladder removal life.

Ultimately, the role of fiber extends beyond mere physical health; it is a critical component of a dietary strategy designed to support not only your digestion but also your life's quality in the long term. By embracing fiber in your diet, you're not just eating smarter; you're investing in a foundation of health that will support you throughout your life's journey.

Chapter 4: Meal Planning Strategies

Embarking on a dietary journey without a gallbladder can feel a bit daunting at first, especially when faced with the dual challenge of meeting your nutritional needs while managing a hectic lifestyle. This is where the art of meal planning emerges not just as a survival skill, but as a transformative practice, turning the seemingly mundane task of weekly menu crafting into a powerful tool for health and wellness.

Imagine this: It's a crisp Monday morning and instead of facing the usual chaos of unplanned meals and last-minute dining decisions, you have a clear roadmap of what to eat for the week. Not only do you dodge the discomfort of inappropriate food choices, but your body, already attuned to a new rhythm without your gallbladder, is nurtured with precisely what it needs to thrive. Meal planning is that peace of mind—knowing that your meals will support, not sabotage, your sensitive digestive system.

In this chapter, we delve deep into creating a balanced weekly menu, a cornerstone of managing a no-gallbladder diet. Each planned meal is like a thread in a beautiful tapestry, contributing to a larger picture of your health. We explore how to efficiently stock your pantry with staples that cater to your specific dietary needs, ensuring that each ingredient serves a purpose, nourishing and healing. Moreover, the tips and tricks shared here are designed to streamline your meal prep process, saving you time and reducing the stress that often comes with last-minute meal decisions.

By adopting meal planning as a habit, you not only ensure that your diet is aligned with your health goals but also reclaim the joy of eating. Each dish, carefully chosen and prepared, becomes a celebration of flavor and an act of self-care. So, let's start this chapter by transforming the necessary task of eating into an enjoyable and healthful ritual that fits seamlessly into the rhythm of your everyday life, ensuring that every meal nourishes and delights, just as it should.

As we step into the practice of creating a balanced weekly menu, we embark on a narrative much like planning a delightful journey. This strategic yet flexible roadmap ensures that every meal is not only a pleasure but a health-giving experience, particularly in the unique circumstances following the removal of your gall er.

Imagine sitting down on a quiet Sunday afternoon with a cup of tea in hand, ready to sketch out the forthcoming week's meals. This scene isn't just about filling slots in a calendar; it's about scripting the week's nutritional story, ensuring each chapter supports the next in a coherent, health-promoting sequence.

The Foundation of Balance

Creating a balance means more than just choosing a variety of foods—it's about making intelligent combinations that maximize nutritional uptake, especially crucial without a gallbladder. Consider this: proteins might pair better with fibrous vegetables to aid slower digestion and reduced strain on your system, while healthy fats, though essential, are best used sparingly and wisely due to your body's modified fat digestion capabilities.

Diversity with Purpose

Diversity on the plate ensures you cover a broad spectrum of nutrients. Each type of nutrient has a role, from minerals and vitamins to proteins and carbohydrates that your body needs to function optimally. However, diversity should also consider taste and texture, making meals more appealing and ensuring that eating remains a joy, not a chore. Think of a color palette; just as a painter mixes hues to capture the right mood, so too will you mix flavors, colors, and textures to create a satisfying dietary mosaic.

Mindful Day Partitioning

Think of your eating day as divided into strategic segments where each meal and snack has a role in a finely tuned symphony of nutrition. Breakfasts could be light yet fiber-rich, easing the body out of fasting mode without overwhelming it. Lunches might prioritize lean proteins and grains that provide steady energy for the afternoon. Dinners, meanwhile, could be gentle yet filling, prefacing a night of restorative sleep. Within this framework, snacks are tactically placed to maintain blood sugar levels and prevent the sudden hunger that can lead to poor food choices.

Strategic Ingredient Integration

Considering you have no gallbladder, the choice of ingredients in your meals must be strategic. Foods naturally low in fat and rich in essential nutrients that support liver health and bile regulation should form the backbone of your diet plans. Ingredients like beetroot, cucumbers, and leafy greens are not just nutritious; they also help in creating meals that are both healing and satisfying.

Flexibility Meets Structure

While consistency is crucial, especially when regulating a sensitive digestive system, incorporating flexibility in your weekly menu confers many benefits. For example, if Wednesday is typically a hectic day, planning simpler meals or utilizing slow-cooker recipes can relieve stress without sacrificing nutritional quality. Similarly, the spontaneous inclusion of seasonal vegetables can inject unexpected variety and freshness into your diet, keeping meals exciting and nutritionally optimized.

Synchronous Cooking

When crafting your weekly menu, think about how certain meals can serve multiple purposes. Cooking a larger batch of quinoa on Monday can save time by becoming a side on Tuesday and a salad base on Wednesday. This strategy, often called batch cooking, is both time-efficient and supportive of dietary consistency, crucial for someone managing a delicate digestive system post-gallbladder removal.

Anticipation and Adjustments

Effective meal planning also involves looking forward and making adjustments based on last week's experiences. Did a particular meal leave you feeling unwell or particularly good? Use these cues to tailor the upcoming week, learning constantly about what best fuels your body and what to avoid.

The Role of Supplements

In some cases, your doctor might recommend supplements to ensure you receive adequate bile acids to help digest fats or other dietary supplements to support your health. Integrating these into your meal plan—considering their timing and potential interactions with meals—is also a part of creating your balanced menu.

Portion Control

It's not just what you eat; it's also how much. Without a gallbladder, large meals can be particularly taxing. Plan for smaller, more frequent eating occasions, which can prevent overwhelming your system and support better digestion and nutrient absorption.

Empowering Yourself Through Education

Understanding the 'why' behind each food choice can empower and motivate you to stick to your meal plan. Educate yourself about the properties of various foods and how they intersect with your body's specific needs. This knowledge makes the meal planning process less of a task and more a fulfilling journey in self-care.

Bringing Joy Back to the Table

Finally, remember that food is not just fuel. It's a source of pleasure, a way to connect with loved they bring us each day. By crafting a thoughtful and balanced weekly menu, you are paving the way for not just functional eating, but joyous, delightful meals that look after your body while feeding your soul.

In this structured yet flexible approach to meal planning, you find not just the route to better health post-gallbladder surgery but a rhythm of eating that feels natural, supportive, and deeply satisfying. Through thoughtful preparation, each meal becomes a stepping stone to a healthier, happier you.

4.2 SHOPPING LISTS AND PANTRY STAPLES

The foundation of any successful meal plan, especially for those navigating the dietary waters after gallbladder removal, lays in the well-stocked pantry and an intelligently crafted shopping list. Think of this as painting a masterpiece; just as an artist requires the right palette of colors to bring their vision to life, so too do you need the right array of ingredients to ensure your nutritional canvas is both beautiful and beneficial.

The Art of the List

Creating a shopping list is an art in proactive preparation. It's not merely jotting down items as you run out; it's about anticipating your body's needs, reflecting on the meal plan, and ensuring each ingredient promotes a gentle digestion process and enriches your health. When you enter the grocery store with a list in hand, you're not just shopping; you're curating the elements of your well-being.

The list should serve as a map, guiding you through each aisle with purpose and preventing the all-too-common impulse buys that might not align with your dietary needs. Each item on your list corresponds to planned meals and their nutritional intent, ensuring you gather everything you need in one trip and avoid the temptation of foods that could disrupt your delicately balanced diet.

Prioritizing Pantry Staples

A pantry well-stocked with the right staples is like a treasure chest that equips you to handle any meal with ease and assurance. For those without a gallbladder, this means staples that are low in fats and easy on digestion but still rich in flavor and nutritional value.

- **Whole Grains**: Quinoa, brown rice, and rolled oats, for example, are not only versatile but their high fiber content helps manage digestion and sustain energy levels.
- **Lean Proteins**: Canned or dried beans, lentils, and chickpeas; pouches of water-packed tuna or salmon. These sources are invaluable for their protein without the high fat content that can be challenging to digest.
- **Low-Fat Dairy Alternatives**: Stock almond, oat, or coconut milk as delightful substitutes that are gentle on the stomach and can be used in everything from morning cereals to creamy sauces.
- **Spices and Herbs**: Herbs and spices are miraculous in their dual role of flavoring and healing. Turmeric, for instance, offers anti-inflammatory properties, while ginger can help ease digestive discomfort.
- **Healthy Fats**: Even without a gall bladder, your body still needs fats, just in more manageable forms. Avocado oil, olive oil, and small portions of nuts or seeds can enrich your meals without overwhelming your system.
- **Vegetables and Fruits**: Stock a variety of fresh or frozen vegetables and fruits. These not only provide essential vitamins and minerals but their fiber-rich nature supports digestive health.

Strategic Shopping

Navigating the grocery store with a gallbladder-friendly perspective is crucial. Start by encircling the outer aisles, which typically house the freshest ingredients—fruits, vegetables, lean meats, and dairy alternatives. The inner aisles hold pantry essentials but also pose temptations with processed foods which are often high in unhealthy fats and additives; approach them with discernment, focusing on your list and your health objectives.

Quality Over Quantity

When it comes to ingredients, quality can significantly influence how your body handles them. Organic produce, lean cuts of meat, and low-fat dairy products are preferable. These might come with a higher price tag, but considering the cost of discomfort and health complications that inappropriate foods might entail, they are an investment in your health.

Moreover, consider the economic efficiency of buying certain items in bulk—whole grains and dried beans, for instance, which have long shelf lives and are staples of your diet. These purchases reduce the frequency of shopping trips and ensure you always have basic building blocks for healthy meals at hand.

The Rhythm of Shopping

Incorporate grocery shopping into your weekly routine at a time when you feel most energetic and least rushed. Perhaps this becomes a Saturday morning ritual after breakfast, setting a positive and proactive tone for the week ahead. The rhythm of regular shopping trips not only aids in meal consistency but also in budget management, as you're less likely to find yourself resorting to expensive last-minute meals or unhealthy takeout.

Closing Thoughts

As you transform your shopping list and pantry staples from mere food sources to guardians of your digestive health, you craft not just meals but a lifestyle attuned to the unique needs of life post-gallbladder removal. Through thoughtful selection and strategic shopping, you empower yourself with control over what you consume, ensuring that each ingredient supports your journey toward digestive health and overall well-being.

Remember, the goal is not just to fill a pantry or complete a shopping list; it's to craft a toolkit that builds, nourishes, and sustains your body, turning every meal into an opportunity for health and happiness. This way, the act of shopping itself becomes not just a necessity, but an integral part of your healing and health maintenance strategy.

Entering the kitchen for meal prep can be much like setting the stage for a performance. Each actor (ingredient) must know their part, and every scene (meal) needs to be meticulously planned for a show(stopping dining experience that is both nutritious and gentle on a digestive system adjusting to life without a gallbladder. This part of your dietary journey is about transforming raw ingredients into nourishing, simple, and digestible meals that can be conveniently assembled throughout the week.

Understanding the Basics of Meal Prep

Meal preparation is more than just cooking; it's an orchestrated effort to make your weekly eating plan work seamlessly with your lifestyle. It involves selecting the right ingredients, cooking them in ways that preserve or enhance their nutritional content, and storing them safely and conveniently. This process helps streamline your daily cooking needs, reduces waste, and ensures that you have healthy options readily available, thereby avoiding the temptation of less suitable, impromptu meals easily triggered by stress or a tight schedule.

Strategic Cooking Sessions

Think of your cooking session as a strategic operation. Starting with proteins, consider baking, grilling, or steaming large batches of chicken, fish, or tofu. These methods are not only simple and quick but also allow for better fat management, which is crucial in a no-gallbladder diet. Once cooked, these proteins can be cooled, portioned, and stored in the refrigerator or freezer, ready to be the star in various meals throughout the week. For grains and legumes, such as quinoa, rice, or lentils, cooking in bulk saves time and energy. These can be cooked with just water or a low-fat broth to enhance their flavor without adding unnecessary fats. Once prepared, they provide a hearty base for salads, soups, or as sides for your main dishes.

Vegetables in the Mix

Vegetables can be prepped once for use in multiple meals. Washing, chopping, and storing them in clear containers not only makes them easily accessible but also more likely to be used. Roasting a large tray of mixed vegetables like carrots, zucchini, and bell peppers with minimal oil and herbs can create a versatile mix ready to add to wraps, omelets, or as a flavorful side.

Dressings and Sauces

Creating your own dressings and sauces can greatly enhance the enjoyment and digestibility of your meals. Using ingredients like yogurt, herbs, vinegar, and citrus juice can produce delicious toppings that add moisture and flavor without the heavy fats that are tough on your system.

Smart Storage Solutions

Efficient storage is key to maintaining the freshness and nutritional quality of your prepped meals. Use glass containers as they do not retain odors or flavors and allow you to see what's inside easily. Labeling containers with the date and contents can help you keep track of what you have and ensure that nothing is forgotten or wasted.

Thawing and Reheating

Part of meal prep's beauty lies in its ability to let you prepare meals ahead of time. However, this means you'll often need to thaw and reheat food. Always thaw foods in the refrigerator overnight rather than at room temperature to keep them safe from bacterial growth. When reheating, ensure that the food is heated thoroughly to the right temperature, making it safe to eat and helping regain a pleasant texture.

The Power of Smoothies and Shakes

For those rushed mornings or afternoons when you need a quick yet nutritious option, prepped smoothies or shakes can be a lifesaver. Preparing individual servings of fruits, greens, and protein powders in bags and storing them in the freezer allows for a quick blend with your choice of milk or water.

Routine Establishment

Just like any other beneficial habit, meal prep thrives on routine. Setting aside a specific day and time each week for meal prep not only fosters a habit but also mentally prepares you for the task, making it less daunting and more a part of your normal weekly rhythm.

Adapt and Overcome

Lastly, always remember to be flexible and adaptive. No matter how well you plan, there will be days when things don't go as expected. Maybe you'll find you're not in the mood for what you've prepared, or perhaps an ingredient didn't hold up as well as you hoped. Use these moments as opportunities to tweak your process and learn what works best for your lifestyle and dietary needs.

Meal prep, with its many facets, is an empowering tool in your no-gallbladder diet toolkit. It not only saves time and reduces stress but also ensures that your nutritional needs are met with every meal. By dedicating time to prepare, you're investing in your health and ensuring that each meal supports your digestion and overall wellbeing with kindness and efficiency. As you grow more comfortable in this practice, you'll likely find that meal prep becomes not just a helpful strategy but a rewarding part of your wellness journey.

CHAPTER 5: LIFESTYLE AND DIETARY ADJUSTMENTS

Adjusting to a life without your gallbladder doesn't mean you have to pause your social activities or compromise on the joy of dining out. Indeed, while it may require some alterations to how you approach meals away from the comfort of your own kitchen, the art of maintaining a rich and adaptable lifestyle is entirely attainable.

Imagine you're planning a vibrant evening out with friends or setting off on a weekend getaway. The thought of navigating menus or finding suitable food choices might seem daunting. However, with the right strategies and mindset, these situations can transform into opportunities for further embracing your new dietary lifestyle. This chapter is crafted to not only ease those concerns but also to enrich your understanding and mastery over your eating habits in every scenario—be it a cozy family dinner out, a business lunch, or a spontaneous road trip.

Let's delve into how simple practices, such my personal favorite step of preemptively browsing restaurant menus or carrying a small snack pouch, can safeguard your digestive health while letting you relish the culinary delights. You'd be surprised how many eateries are accommodating to special dietary needs when given a heads up!

Moreover, I'll share some personal anecdotes and successes that underscore the importance of balance. For instance, learning to identify which lighter food combinations can both satisfy your taste buds and suit your post-surgery body is an invaluable skill. It's not just about avoiding certain fats or large meals; it's about relearning and trusting your body's signals, which can guide your choices towards optimal health and dining pleasure.

Life post-gallbladder surgery is an ongoing journey of learning and adaptation – one that, with the right knowledge and adjustments, can be as enjoyable, if not more so, than before. Remember, each plate is a palette, and every meal is an opportunity to paint your path towards a healthier you with delectable, carefully-chosen colors.

5.1 EATING OUT WITHOUT A GALLBLADDER

Navigating the wide world of dining out can often feel like charting a course through unknown waters, especially when you're doing so without a gallbladder. The challenge isn't just about avoiding discomfort; it's about discovering ways to enjoy vibrant social interactions and delicious meals without the shadow of dietary distress looming over you.

Let's recount a tale of two dinners. Picture this: During the first outing, you find yourself at a lavish Italian restaurant with friends. The menu is tempting with creamy pastas and rich pizzas. Caught up in the moment (and a lack of preparation), you choose a dish that sounds light but is secretly laden with fats and oils. The immediate gratification is shadowed by hours of discomfort. Now, imagine a different scenario where you've planned ahead. You've contacted the restaurant beforehand, previewed the menu online, and prepared questions for the waiter. You select a dish tailored to your needs, perhaps a delightful grilled fish with steamed vegetables, and you end the meal not only satisfied but also symptom-free.

These examples aren't just stories; they are common experiences for those adjusting to life post-gallbladder surgery. The key difference lies in the approach and preparation. Here are comprehensive strategies to make eating out a joyful and comfortable experience.

Understanding Restaurant Menus

Menus are your first clue to understanding what's safe for you to eat. However, they can also be misleading. Words like "baked" or "grilled" might suggest a healthier option but don't reveal the use of heavy marinades or cooking oils. Developing a habit of reading between the lines can be your greatest tool. Look for dishes with clear descriptions and don't hesitate to ask how they are prepared. Chefs often cater to dietary restrictions and might offer to prepare a dish that accommodates your needs.

Communicating with Staff

Never underestimate the power of communication. Upon arrival, or better yet when you book your table, inform the restaurant of your dietary requirements. Most establishments are eager to provide a good experience and can offer valuable insights into their menu options. A simple conversation with your server can shield you from ingredients that might trigger symptoms, such a high-fat dressings or fried garnishes.

Choosing the Right Restaurants

Not all dining environments are created equal when it comes to accommodating post-gallbladder diets. Ethnic cuisines such as Japanese, Mediterranean, or Indian often offer a wide range of suitable dishes that emphasize grains, legumes, and lean meats. On the other hand, establishments known for their rich, creamy, or deep-fried foods might require more careful navigation. Opting for restaurants that focus on fresh ingredients and minimalistic cooking styles can significantly enhance your dining experience.

Portion Control

Restaurants are notorious for serving generous portions, which can spell trouble for someone managing a sensitive digestive system. Instead of settling for the default quantity, consider ordering a starter as your main course, or sharing a larger dish with a friend. This way, you can enjoy a variety of flavors without overwhelming your system.

Handling Social Implications

Eating out is as much a social ritual as it is a nutritional necessity, and explaining your dietary restrictions to dining companions might feel cumbersome. However, embracing this as part place of your new normal can empower you and even educate others about being mindful eaters. Most friends and family will be supportive once they understand your needs, turning potentially awkward moments into opportunities for shared learning.

Staying Flexible and Positive

Despite best efforts, there might be occasions where options are limited, and you have to make the best out of what's available. Keeping a flexible mindset allows you to adjust without feeling frustrated or deprived. Remember, the goal is not just to eat within strict guidelines but to enjoy life's pleasures—including food.

Preparing for the Unpredictable

Always carry a small "emergency" snack in your bag—something simple and safe, like a small packet of almonds or a piece of fruit. This can be a lifesaver when options are less than ideal, or meals are delayed.

Learning from Each Experience

Each dining experience offers valuable insights into what works and what doesn't for your body. Maintain a diary or a mental log of foods and restaurants that suit you well and those that don't. Over time, this record will make it easier to make quick, informed dining choices without the stress or worry of adverse reactions.

The journey of dining out without a gallbladder is much like any other aspect of life post-surgery—it's about adaptation, not limitation. By equipping yourself with knowledge, preparing ahead, and choosing your dining environment wisely, you can transform eating out from a source of anxiety into an enjoyable, and even adventurous part of your life. Remember, each meal out is not just a chance to nourish your body, but also to celebrate your resilience and embrace your new lifestyle with gusto.

5.2 TRAVEL TIPS FOR SPECIAL DIETS

Embarking on a journey, whether it's a leisurely vacation or a quick business trip, can bring a mixture of excitement and anxiety for anyone managing a post-gallbladder removal diet. The unpredictable nature of travel foods, coupled with the challenge of finding suitable meal options on the go, might seem daunting. Yet, with thoughtful planning and the right strategies, you can roam far and wide without digestive distress, meeting new cultures and cuisines with confidence and ease.

Envision this: you're about to take off on a long-awaited overseas journey. You've done your homework, planning each meal with precision, yet there's a twinge of worry about what you'll eat when the airplane meal rolls out, or when you're faced with exotic local dishes. Here's how to navigate these new culinary waters gracefully, keeping your health and comfort at the forefront.

Pre-Trip Planning

Just like a skilled navigator charts their course before setting sail, laying the groundwork before your trip can make all the difference. Start by researching your destination. Look into local dining customs, typical food ingredients, and available eating establishments. Many countries are increasingly aware of dietary restrictions and offer alternatives for special diets. Websites and travel forums can offer insights and restaurant recommendations from fellow travelers with similar dietary needs.

If you're booked in a hotel, contact them ahead of your stay to discuss your dietary requirements. Many hotels are well-equipped to cater to special diets, offering meal options that can be tailored to your needs. Knowing that suitable food will be available upon arrival can ease a great deal of travel anxiety.

Packing Essentials

While traveling light is often advised, when it concerns your dietary health, packing a few essential items can be a lifesaver. Include snacks that are compliant with your post-gallbladder removal diet—nuts, seeds, low-fat granola bars, or digestive-friendly fruits like bananas. These can be lifesavers during long flights, layovers, or when suitable food options are scarce.

Moreover, consider packing a small travel kit with digestive aids—perhaps herbal teas known to support digestion, or over-the-counter supplements that aid in breaking down fats. Don't forget to pack any medications you regularly need as well.

On the Go

Air travel, in particular, requires strategic eating. Airplane food is often high in fats and sugars, which can be harsh on a sensitive digestive system. You can request special meals when booking your flight—most airlines offer a variety of dietary options that cater to restrictions like low-fat or gluten-free. Alternatively, consider eating a hearty meal before your flight, allowing you to skip the airplane food altogether in favor of your packed snacks.

When you're exploring your destination, look for grocery stores or local markets near your accommodation. They can be great sources for fresh produce and other foods that fit your diet. You might even find new digestive-friendly foods that you hadn't considered before.

Dining Out

Eating out in a foreign country can be one of the joys of travel. To navigate this joyfully and safely, choose restaurants that have a reputation for quality and that offer transparency in their ingredients. Many eating places provide English menus or have staff who can help translate the menu for you. Don't hesitate to ask questions about the ingredients and the preparation methods used.

Embracing Local Cuisine

Exploring local cuisine is a delightful aspect of travel but requires cautious enthusiasm. Educate yourself on typical dishes and their ingredients common in the region. Often, you can find local specialties that are not only safe but will introduce you to new flavors and preparations that naturally comply with a low-fat, gentle diet.

For instance, in Japan, a meal of sashimi (fresh, thinly sliced raw fish), rice, and miso soup offers a flavorful, low-fat dining experience. In Mediterranean regions, dishes like grilled seafood, salads drizzled with olive oil, and plenty of fresh vegetables can cater well to your dietary needs.

Managing Unexpected Challenges

Despite the best laid plans, travel can often present unexpected challenges. You might find yourself in a situation where your dietary options are limited, or communication difficulties make it hard to ascertain food ingredients. In such cases, opting for the simplest dishes, such as steamed vegetables, rice, or grilled proteins, can be a safe choice. Carrying a dietary card in the local language, which explains your dietary restrictions, can also assist in communicating your needs effectively.

Reflecting and Learning

Every trip is a learning experience. Reflect on what worked well and what you could improve for next time. Perhaps you found a snack that was particularly effective in curbing hunger without causing discomfort, or maybe you discovered a restaurant chain that caters to suitable meal options.

Traveling without a gallbladder is undoubtedly an adventure in itself—a chance to explore not only new landscapes but also the boundaries of your dietary resilience. Armed with the right preparation, a curious and flexible attitude, and a well-packed snack bag, you can ensure that your travel experiences are as enriching and comforting as they are exciting.

5.3 MANAGING STRESS AND ITS IMPACT ON DIGESTION

Managing stress becomes particularly crucial when you're adapting to life without a gallbladder. The connection between stress and digestive health is profoundly interlinked, a chorus where the mind and gut often sing together, albeit not always harmoniously. For those navigating the delicate dance of digestion post-gallbladder removal, understanding and managing stress is not just beneficial; it's essential for maintaining overall wellbeing. Consider a familiar scenario – you are preparing for an important work presentation, and the tension builds. Your stomach churns and twinges of discomfort remind you of the delicate ecosystem within. This isn't mere coincidence; it's your body reacting to stress in a very physical way. The nervous system and digestive system are so closely connected that the state of one significantly affects the other. So, managing stress isn't simply about feeling better mentally but also about allowing your digestive system to perform optimally.

The Impact of Stress on Digestion

Stress triggers the release of various hormones and chemicals like cortisol and adrenaline, which prepare your body for the so-called 'fight or flight' response. While these reactions are life-saving in acute situations, chronic stress can lead to a host of digestive problems. In people without a gallbladder, these issues can be exacerbated due to the direct impact on bile flow and fat digestion. Symptoms like bloating, cramps, indigestion, or irregular bowel movements can all be aggravated by unmanaged stress.

Techniques for Stress Management

Rediscovering harmony within your digestive system involves adopting effective stress management techniques. These strategies can range from mindfulness exercises to structured physical activities, all aimed at reducing the psychological pressures that may inflame gastrointestinal symptoms.

Mindfulness and Relaxation Techniques: Mindfulness meditation, yoga, or even simple breathing exercises can significantly reduce stress levels. These practices help shift your body's balance from stress-inducing hormone production to a more relaxed state, supporting smoother digestion. Engaging regularly in these activities can also enhance your awareness of how your body reacts to stress, giving you better cues for early intervention.

Regular Physical Activity: Exercise isn't just vital for overall health; it's also a potent stress reliever. Activities such as walking, swimming, or cycling can help reduce the levels of the body's stress hormones and stimulate the production of endorphins, the brain's feel-good neurotransmitters. Moreover, regular exercise can help normalize and regulate bowel movements, which can often become irregular during periods of high stress.

Adequate Sleep: Never underestimate the power of a good night's sleep in managing stress. Sleep deprivation can exacerbate stress and thus negatively impact digestive health. Establishing a regular, soothing bedtime routine and aiming for 7 to 9 hours of sleep per night can help maintain both mental and gastrointestinal health.

Cognitive Behavioral Therapy (CBT)

For chronic stress, more structured support like cognitive behavioral therapy (CBT) can be beneficial. CBT is a type of psychotherapy that helps individuals manage problems by changing the way they think and behave. It teaches stress management skills by helping you understand the relationship between your mindset and your physical symptoms.

Building a Supportive Environment

Creating a supportive social environment is also crucial in managing stress. Strong relationships and social networks provide emotional support, reduce feelings of isolation, and can directly impact your ability to handle stress. Whether it's close family members, friends, or support groups for those without a gallbladder, staying connected provides a buffer against stress.

Diet and Nutritional Support

While this discussion intersects with earlier dietary considerations covered in this book, it bears repeating that what you eat impacts how you feel. Consuming a balanced diet rich in antioxidants, vitamins, and minerals can support the nervous system and mitigate some of the impacts of stress. Moreover, small, frequent meals can prevent the digestive discomforts that might arise from eating large meals under stress, which can be particularly challenging without a gallbladder.

Addressing Professional Needs

Sometimes, stress is rooted in professional dissatisfaction or workplace challenges. It may be worth considering professional counseling or even career-oriented interventions if your job is a significant source of stress. A fulfilling professional life can promote overall happiness and significantly reduce daily stress levels.

The Role of Routine

Finally, establishing a routine can play a pivotal role in stress reduction. Routines create a sense of order to your day that can make life appear less chaotic. Within this structure, designate time for meals, exercise, relaxation, and sleep. Knowing what to expect can tame the chaos, helping to ease both your mind and your gut.

In conclusion, managing stress is not just about coping with the mental strains of daily life but about nurturing a digestive system that requires gentle handling post-gallbladder surgery. Each strategy enhances another, creating a comprehensive approach to health that supports both your emotional and physical well-being. Remember, the journey to recovery and adaptation is not just about what you eat but also about how you think, react, and live day-to-day.

Chapter 6: Breakfast Recipes

Welcome to the comforting embrace of breakfast, the most essential yet often the most neglected meal of the day, especially when navigating life after gallbladder surgery. For many, morning heralds a rush of activities, setting the stage for hurried meals that barely satisfy or sit well with your new digestive needs. Yet, what if I told you that breakfast could become a haven of nourishment and delight, setting a positive tone for the rest of your day?

In this chapter, we explore breakfast recipes designed to be gentle on your digestion while tantalizing your taste buds. Imagine starting your day with a smoothie or shake that blends the creamy textures of bananas and the rich, subtle sweetness of almond milk, infused with a dash of honey—easy on the stomach and delightful to the senses. Or consider the cozy, comforting warmth of oatmeal simmered in cinnamon and topped with a sprinkle of digestive-friendly chia seeds, offering you a fiber-rich start with just the right amount of sweetness.

The journey of adapting to a no gallbladder diet need not be a flavorless one. Through thoughtful ingredient selection and preparation methods tailored for your condition, these breakfast options are crafted to prevent discomfort and provide essential nutrients without overwhelming your system. They offer a variety of flavors and textures, from the gentle simplicity of porridge to the satisfying complexity of an egg-based dish that features spices and herbs known for their anti-inflammatory properties.

These recipes are not just about avoiding pain or discomfort—they are about rediscovering the joy of breakfast. Whether you have a few extra minutes to prepare an egg scramble with a variety of fresh vegetables or need to blend a quick shake before dashing out the door, my goal is to bring you back to a place where breakfast is not just the first meal of the day but a cherished ritual that supports your digestion and lifts your spirits.

As we move through this chapter, I invite you to embrace these recipes as your stepping-stones to a day full of energy and free from discomfort, transforming everyday eating into a healing, rejuvenating process that you look forward to each morning.

6.1 Smoothies and Shakes

Tropical Mango and Turmeric Smoothie

Preparation Time: 10 min.
Cooking Time: none
Mode of Cooking: Blending
Servings: 2

Ingredients:

- 1 cup frozen mango chunks
- 1 small banana
- 1 cup coconut water
- ½ tsp ground turmeric
- 1 tsp honey
- 1 Tbsp chia seeds
- Juice of ½ lime

Directions:

1. Combine mango, banana, coconut water, turmeric, honey, chia seeds, and lime juice in a blender
2. Blend until smooth and creamy
3. Pour into glasses and serve immediately

Tips:

- Add a pinch of black pepper to enhance turmeric absorption

- Can substitute honey with maple syrup for a different sweetness

Nutritional Values: Calories: 155, Fat: 1g, Carbs: 36g, Protein: 2g, Sugar: 28g, Sodium: 42 mg, Potassium: 487 mg, Cholesterol: 0 mg

GREEN APPLE AND SPINACH DETOX SHAKE

Preparation Time: 8 min.
Cooking Time: none
Mode of Cooking: Blending
Servings: 1
Ingredients:

- 1 green apple, cored and sliced
- 1 cup fresh spinach
- 1 celery stalk, chopped
- ½ cucumber, sliced
- 1 cup almond milk, unsweetened
- 1 Tbsp fresh mint leaves
- Juice of 1 lemon

Directions:

1. Place all ingredients into a blender
2. Blend on high until smooth
3. Serve chilled for a refreshing detox boost

Tips:

- Use organic ingredients to avoid pesticide residues
- Increase or decrease almond milk to adjust consistency

Nutritional Values: Calories: 120, Fat: 2g, Carbs: 25g, Protein: 3g, Sugar: 14g, Sodium: 85 mg, Potassium: 567 mg, Cholesterol: 0 mg

BERRY BEETROOT BLAST SMOOTHIE

Preparation Time: 12 min.
Cooking Time: none
Mode of Cooking: Blending
Servings: 2
Ingredients:

- ½ cup cooked beetroot, chopped
- 1 cup mixed berries (strawberries, blueberries, raspberries)
- 1 banana
- 1 cup water
- 1 Tbsp flaxseeds
- 1 tsp vanilla extract

Directions:

1. Combine beetroot, mixed berries, banana, water, flaxseeds, and vanilla extract in a blender
2. Blend until smooth
3. Serve in tall glasses adorned with a berry skewer

Tips:

- Freeze berries in advance to make the smoothie colder and thicker
- Beetroot can be roasted or boiled prior to use for smoother blending

Nutritional Values: Calories: 130, Fat: 2g, Carbs: 28g, Protein: 3g, Sugar: 16g, Sodium: 58 mg, Potassium: 421 mg, Cholesterol: 0 mg

VANILLA ALMOND PROTEIN SMOOTHIE

Preparation Time: 10 min.
Cooking Time: none
Mode of Cooking: Blending
Servings: 2
Ingredients:

- 1 cup unsweetened almond milk
- 1 scoop vanilla protein powder, low-fat
- 1 frozen banana, sliced
- 2 Tbsp almond butter
- 1 Tbsp chia seeds
- ½ tsp vanilla extract
- Ice cubes as needed

Directions:

1. Combine all ingredients in a blender and blend on high until smooth and creamy
2. Pour into glasses and serve immediately

Tips:

- Use frozen banana to thicken the smoothie without ice for a creamier texture
- Add a pinch of cinnamon for an extra flavor boost
- If the smoothie is too thick, adjust consistency with additional almond milk

Nutritional Values: Calories: 265, Fat: 9g, Carbs: 30g, Protein: 18g, Sugar: 12g, Sodium: 180 mg, Potassium: 450 mg, Cholesterol: 5 mg

BERRY BLAST PROTEIN SHAKE

Preparation Time: 8 min.
Cooking Time: none
Mode of Cooking: Blending
Servings: 2
Ingredients:
- 1 cup fresh strawberries, hulled
- ½ cup blueberries
- 1 scoop low-fat strawberry or plain protein powder
- ¾ cup low-fat Greek yogurt
- 1 Tbsp flaxseed, ground
- ½ cup water
- Ice cubes as desired

Directions:
1. Place all ingredients except ice into the blender
2. Blend until smooth
3. Add ice cubes and blend to desired consistency

Tips:
- Experiment with different berries like raspberries or blackberries to vary flavor and nutrient profile
- Add a teaspoon of honey if more sweetness is desired
- Incorporate a handful of spinach for an extra nutritional boost without altering taste significantly

Nutritional Values: Calories: 220, Fat: 3g, Carbs: 28g, Protein: 20g, Sugar: 16g, Sodium: 65 mg, Potassium: 320 mg, Cholesterol: 10 mg

PEANUT BUTTER BANANA PROTEIN SMOOTHIE

Preparation Time: 7 min.
Cooking Time: none
Mode of Cooking: Blending
Servings: 1
Ingredients:
- 1 large banana
- 1 Tbsp peanut butter, unsweetened and low-fat
- ½ cup oat milk
- 1 scoop chocolate protein powder, low-fat
- ½ cup ice cubes
- 1 tsp honey, optional

Directions:
1. Blend the banana, peanut butter, oat milk, and chocolate protein powder until smooth
2. Add ice cubes and blend again until the desired thickness is reached

Tips:
- Opt for natural peanut butter with no added sugars or oils for healthier fat content
- A dash of vanilla extract enhances the peanut butter flavor
- If a thinner smoothie is preferred, gradually add more oat milk while blending

Nutritional Values: Calories: 345, Fat: 10g, Carbs: 40g, Protein: 25g, Sugar: 22g, Sodium: 190 mg, Potassium: 480 mg, Cholesterol: 5 mg

BERRY BEET MORNING BLISS

Preparation Time: 10 min.
Cooking Time: none
Mode of Cooking: Blending
Servings: 2
Ingredients:
- 1/2 cup cooked beets, peeled and chopped
- 1 cup mixed berries (strawberries, blueberries, raspberries), fresh or frozen
- 1 small banana
- 1 cup spinach leaves
- 1 Tbsp chia seeds
- 1 1/2 cups almond milk, unsweetened

Directions:
1. Place beets, mixed berries, banana, spinach, chia seeds, and almond milk in a blender
2. Blend on high until smooth and creamy
3. Pour into glasses and serve immediately

Tips:
- Add a tsp of flaxseed oil for an omega-3 boost

- If the smoothie is too thick, adjust consistency with additional almond milk

Nutritional Values: Calories: 150, Fat: 3g, Carbs: 28g, Protein: 4g, Sugar: 16g, Sodium: 55 mg, Potassium: 400 mg, Cholesterol: 0 mg

GREEN GINGER GLOW

Preparation Time: 5 min.
Cooking Time: none
Mode of Cooking: Blending
Servings: 1
Ingredients:
- 1 large cucumber, peeled and sliced
- 1/2 ripe avocado
- 1 cup kale, stems removed
- 1/2 apple, cored and chopped
- 1-inch piece of ginger, peeled and minced
- 1 cup coconut water
- Juice of 1/2 lemon

Directions:

1. Combine cucumber, avocado, kale, apple, ginger, coconut water, and lemon juice in a blender
2. Blend until smooth and vibrant green
3. Taste and adjust flavor with more lemon or ginger if necessary

Tips:
- A pinch of turmeric can be added for anti-inflammatory properties
- Keep skins on apples and cucumbers if they are organic to maximize fiber intake

Nutritional Values: Calories: 180, Fat: 7g, Carbs: 27g, Protein: 3g, Sugar: 14g, Sodium: 30 mg, Potassium: 890 mg, Cholesterol: 0 mg

CARROT PINEAPPLE POWER

Preparation Time: 8 min.
Cooking Time: none
Mode of Cooking: Blending
Servings: 2
Ingredients:
- 2 cups carrot juice, fresh
- 1 cup pineapple chunks, fresh or frozen
- 1/2 cup mango chunks, fresh or frozen
- 1/2 tsp cinnamon
- 1 Tbsp honey (optional)
- Juice of 1 lime

Directions:

1. Add carrot juice, pineapple chunks, mango chunks, cinnamon, honey if using, and lime juice into a blender
2. Blend until smooth
3. Serve chilled for a refreshing morning start

Tips:
- Optional ginger for an extra zing
- Use fresh juice and ripe fruits for the best flavor and nutritional benefits

Nutritional Values: Calories: 160, Fat: 0.5g, Carbs: 39g, Protein: 2g, Sugar: 30g, Sodium: 70 mg, Potassium: 300 mg, Cholesterol: 0 mg

6.2 OATMEAL AND PORRIDGES

QUINOA APPLE CINNAMON PORRIDGE

Preparation Time: 10 min.
Cooking Time: 20 min.
Mode of Cooking: Stovetop
Servings: 2
Ingredients:
- 1 cup rinsed quinoa
- 2 cups water
- 1 medium apple, peeled and diced
- 1 tsp cinnamon
- 1 Tbsp honey
- ¼ cup chopped walnuts
- 1 cup fat-free milk

Directions:

1. Combine quinoa and water in a saucepan and bring to a boil over high heat
2. Reduce to a simmer, cover, and cook until quinoa is tender and water is absorbed, about 15 min.
3. Stir in diced apple, cinnamon, honey, and walnuts and cook for an additional 5 min.
4. Remove from heat and stir in fat-free milk

Tips:

- Serve hot and sprinkle with extra cinnamon for enhanced flavor
- Use almond milk for a nuttier flavor and lactose-free option

Nutritional Values: Calories: 295, Fat: 4g, Carbs: 55g, Protein: 8g, Sugar: 15g, Sodium: 30mg, Potassium: 429mg, Cholesterol: 2mg

MILLET PUMPKIN PORRIDGE

Preparation Time: 15 min.
Cooking Time: 30 min.
Mode of Cooking: Stovetop
Servings: 3
Ingredients:

- 1 cup millet
- 3 cups water
- 1 cup pureed pumpkin
- 1 tsp vanilla extract
- ½ tsp ground nutmeg
- ½ tsp ground ginger
- 2 Tbsp maple syrup
- 1 Tbsp chia seeds
- 1 cup low-fat coconut milk

Directions:

1. Toast millet in a dry skillet over medium heat until slightly golden, about 3 min.
2. Add water to the skillet and bring to a boil
3. Reduce heat to low, cover, and simmer until millet is soft, about 25 min.
4. Stir in pumpkin puree, spices, maple syrup, and chia seeds and cook for another 5 min.
5. Mix in coconut milk before serving

Tips:

- Top with a dollop of fat-free Greek yogurt for added creaminess
- Sprinkle with pumpkin seeds for extra crunch
- Ensure thorough cooking of millet for optimal digestion

Nutritional Values: Calories: 320, Fat: 5g, Carbs: 62g, Protein: 8g, Sugar: 12g, Sodium: 45mg, Potassium: 401mg, Cholesterol: 0mg

BUCKWHEAT AND BERRY PORRIDGE

Preparation Time: 10 min.
Cooking Time: 15 min.
Mode of Cooking: Stovetop
Servings: 2
Ingredients:

- 1 cup buckwheat groats
- 2 cups water
- 1 cup mixed berries (fresh or frozen)
- 1 tsp ground cinnamon
- 2 Tbsp ground flaxseed
- 1 tsp vanilla extract
- 1 Tbsp honey
- ¼ cup sliced almonds
- 1 cup almond milk

Directions:

1. Rinse buckwheat groats and bring them with water to a boil in a medium saucepan
2. Reduce heat to low, cover, and simmer until buckwheat is tender, about 10 min.
3. Add berries, cinnamon, flaxseed, and vanilla extract and cook for 5 min., stirring occasionally
4. Sweeten with honey and mix in sliced almonds and almond milk before serving

Tips:

- For a smoother texture, blend half of the cooked berries into the porridge
- Serve chilled for a refreshing summer breakfast option
- Almond milk can be substituted with soy milk for a different flavor profile

Nutritional Values: Calories: 335, Fat: 8g, Carbs: 57g, Protein: 9g, Sugar: 16g, Sodium: 15mg, Potassium: 395mg, Cholesterol: 0mg

CINNAMON PEAR BARLEY PORRIDGE

Preparation Time: 10 min
Cooking Time: 30 min
Mode of Cooking: Stove-top
Servings: 2
Ingredients:

- ⅓ cup hulled barley, rinsed

- 1 pear, peeled and diced
- 1½ cups water
- 1 tsp ground cinnamon
- ¼ tsp nutmeg
- 1 Tbsp honey
- ½ cup low-fat milk

Directions:

1. Combine barley and water in a saucepan and bring to a boil
2. Reduce heat to a simmer, cover, and cook until barley is tender, about 25 min
3. Mix in the diced pear, cinnamon, nutmeg, and honey and cook for an additional 5 min
4. Stir in low-fat milk just before serving

Tips:

- Soak barley overnight to reduce cooking time
- Add a pinch of salt to enhance the flavors of the spices
- Serve warm for maximum comfort

Nutritional Values: Calories: 220, Fat: 1.5g, Carbs: 48g, Protein: 6g, Sugar: 16g, Sodium: 30mg, Potassium: 270mg, Cholesterol: 2mg

SAVORY QUINOA AND VEGETABLE PORRIDGE

Preparation Time: 15 min
Cooking Time: 20 min
Mode of Cooking: Stove-top
Servings: 4
Ingredients:

- 1 cup quinoa, rinsed
- 2 cups low-sodium vegetable broth
- 1 carrot, finely diced
- 1 zucchini, finely diced
- ¼ cup diced bell peppers
- 1 tsp olive oil
- ½ tsp turmeric
- 1 Tbsp chopped fresh parsley

Directions:

1. Heat olive oil in a pan and sauté carrots, zucchini, and bell peppers until soft, about 5 min
2. Add quinoa and turmeric, stirring to coat the grains

3. Pour in vegetable broth and bring to a boil, then reduce to a simmer until quinoa is cooked and liquid is absorbed, about 15 min
4. Garnish with fresh parsley before serving

Tips:

- Utilize a variety of vegetables for a nutritional boost
- Quinoa can be substituted with millet for a different texture
- Incorporate a sprinkle of nutritional yeast for a cheesy flavor without the fat

Nutritional Values: Calories: 180, Fat: 3g, Carbs: 30g, Protein: 6g, Sugar: 4g, Sodium: 70mg, Potassium: 410mg, Cholesterol: 0mg

APPLE CINNAMON BUCKWHEAT HOT CEREAL

Preparation Time: 5 min
Cooking Time: 10 min
Mode of Cooking: Stove-top
Servings: 3
Ingredients:

- ½ cup buckwheat groats
- 1 apple, cored and shredded
- 1½ cups water
- 1 tsp ground cinnamon
- 1 Tbsp flaxseed meal
- Honey or maple syrup to taste
- ½ cup almond milk

Directions:

1. Combine buckwheat groats, shredded apple, water, and cinnamon in a pot and bring to a boil
2. Reduce heat and simmer until most of the water is absorbed and groats are tender, about 10 min
3. Stir in flaxseed meal and sweetener to taste
4. Pour almond milk and serve warm

Tips:

- Experiment with different sweeteners like stevia or monk fruit for low-sugar options
- Buckwheat is naturally gluten-free, making it a great option for those with sensitivity

- Add a sprinkle of chia seeds for extra fiber and nutrients

Nutritional Values: Calories: 200, Fat: 2g, Carbs: 41g, Protein: 7g, Sugar: 7g, Sodium: 60mg, Potassium: 150mg, Cholesterol: 0mg

CINNAMON WALNUT OATMEAL

Preparation Time: 5 min
Cooking Time: 10 min
Mode of Cooking: Stovetop
Servings: 2
Ingredients:

- 1 C. rolled oats
- 2 C. water
- 1 pinch salt
- ½ C. chopped walnuts
- 1 tsp ground cinnamon
- 2 Tbsp honey
- ¼ C. flaxseed, ground

Directions:

1. Bring water and salt to a boil in a saucepan
2. Add oats and reduce heat, simmering uncovered for 5 min, stirring occasionally
3. Stir in walnuts, cinnamon, and honey, and cook for another 5 min
4. Remove from heat and stir in ground flaxseed

Tips:

- Serve with a dollop of low-fat yogurt for creaminess without excess fat
- Sprinkle additional cinnamon on top for extra flavor and aroma

Nutritional Values: Calories: 315, Fat: 9g, Carbs: 53g, Protein: 8g, Sugar: 12g, Sodium: 30 mg, Potassium: 240 mg, Cholesterol: 0 mg

PUMPKIN SEED CHIA PORRIDGE

Preparation Time: 10 min
Cooking Time: 20 min
Mode of Cooking: Stovetop
Servings: 2
Ingredients:

- 1/2 C. quinoa
- 1 C. water
- 1 pinch salt
- 1/4 C. pumpkin seeds
- 2 Tbsp chia seeds
- 1/2 tsp vanilla extract
- 1 Tbsp maple syrup
- 1/4 tsp nutmeg

Directions:

1. Rinse quinoa thoroughly and combine with water and salt in a medium saucepan, bring to a boil
2. Reduce to a simmer, cover, and cook until water is absorbed, about 15 min
3. Stir in pumpkin seeds, chia seeds, vanilla extract, maple syrup, and nutmeg, and simmer for an additional 5 min

Tips:

- Top with sliced bananas for a naturally sweet addition
- Chia seeds provide extra fiber, which is important for digestive health

Nutritional Values: Calories: 290, Fat: 8g, Carbs: 45g, Protein: 10g, Sugar: 7g, Sodium: 40 mg, Potassium: 321 mg, Cholesterol: 0 mg

ALMOND SPICE MILLET BOWL

Preparation Time: 10 min
Cooking Time: 25 min
Mode of Cooking: Stovetop
Servings: 2
Ingredients:

- 1/2 C. millet
- 1 1/2 C. water
- 1 pinch salt
- 1/4 C. sliced almonds
- 1/2 tsp cinnamon
- 1/4 tsp cardamom
- 1 Tbsp agave syrup
- 1 Tbsp almond butter

Directions:

1. Rinse millet and combine with water and salt in a saucepan, bring to a boil

2. Reduce heat and simmer covered until millet is tender, about 25 min
3. Stir in almonds, cinnamon, cardamom, agave syrup, and almond butter, cooking until everything is well-blended

Tips:

• Enjoy this dish with a splash of almond milk for added hydration and flavor

• Using almond butter provides a creamy texture without the need for dairy

Nutritional Values: Calories: 310, Fat: 11g, Carbs: 47g, Protein: 8g, Sugar: 4g, Sodium: 30 mg, Potassium: 205 mg, Cholesterol: 0 mg

6.3 EGG-BASED DISHES

SCRAMBLED TOFU WITH SPINACH

Preparation Time: 10 min.
Cooking Time: 10 min.
Mode of Cooking: Sauté
Servings: 2
Ingredients:

• 14 oz. firm tofu, drained and crumbled
• 1 Tbsp olive oil
• 1 cup fresh spinach, rinsed and chopped
• 1 small onion, finely chopped
• 1 clove garlic, minced
• 1 tsp turmeric
• ½ tsp black salt (Kala Namak)
• Fresh herbs (parsley or chives), chopped for garnish

Directions:

1. Heat olive oil in a skillet over medium heat. Add onion and garlic and sauté until soft
2. Add turmeric and black salt to crumbled tofu, mix well, then add this mixture to the skillet
3. Cook for about 5-7 minutes, stirring frequently, until tofu is heated through and slightly golden
4. Stir in spinach and cook until wilted
5. Garnish with fresh herbs before serving

Tips:

• Avoid overcooking the spinach to preserve nutrients

• Adding turmeric not only gives color but supports digestion

• Black salt adds a unique flavor while aiding in digestion

Nutritional Values: Calories: 150, Fat: 9g, Carbs: 8g, Protein: 12g, Sugar: 2g, Sodium: 480 mg, Potassium: 300 mg, Cholesterol: 0 mg

POACHED EGGS OVER ASPARAGUS

Preparation Time: 5 min.
Cooking Time: 8 min.
Mode of Cooking: Boil/Poach
Servings: 2
Ingredients:

• 4 large eggs
• 1 lb. asparagus, ends trimmed
• 1 tsp white vinegar
• Salt and pepper to taste
• Light drizzle of extra virgin olive oil
• 1 Tbsp chopped chives for garnish

Directions:

1. Bring a pot of water with vinegar to a simmer
2. Carefully crack eggs into water and poach for about 3-4 minutes for soft yolks
3. Steam asparagus until tender-crisp, about 4-5 minutes
4. Arrange steamed asparagus on plates, top with poached eggs, season with salt and pepper, drizzle with olive oil, and garnish with chives

Tips:

• Using vinegar in the poaching water helps the egg whites to coalesce more effectively

• Ensure asparagus is not overcooked to maintain nutrient integrity

• Extra virgin olive oil drizzle adds a touch of healthy fats without overwhelming the dish

Nutritional Values: Calories: 123, Fat: 7g, Carbs: 5g, Protein: 10g, Sugar: 2g, Sodium: 210 mg, Potassium: 317 mg, Cholesterol: 186 mg

MUSHROOM AND HERB FRITTATA

Preparation Time: 15 min.
Cooking Time: 25 min.
Mode of Cooking: Bake
Servings: 4
Ingredients:

- 6 large eggs whisked
- ½ cup low-fat milk
- 1 cup mushrooms, thinly sliced
- 1 medium onion, diced
- 1 Tbsp fresh thyme, chopped
- 1 Tbsp fresh rosemary, chopped
- 2 tsp olive oil
- Salt and pepper to taste

Directions:

1. Preheat oven to 375°F (190°C)
2. Heat oil in an oven-safe skillet over medium heat
3. Add onion and mushrooms, cooking until onions are translucent and mushrooms are soft ♫ Add herbs, then pour in eggs mixed with milk, whisking in salt and pepper
4. Cook without stirring for 2 minutes, then place skillet in oven
5. Bake for about 20-23 minutes until frittata is set

Tips:

- Low-fat milk reduces overall fat content without sacrificing texture or flavor
- Herbs like thyme and rosemary add robust flavor without needing excess salt
- Allow to cool for a few minutes before slicing to let the frittata set properly

Nutritional Values: Calories: 140, Fat: 9g, Carbs: 6g, Protein: 9g, Sugar: 4g, Sodium: 220 mg, Potassium: 234 mg, Cholesterol: 430 mg

ZUCCHINI AND TOMATO BASIL OMELETTE

Preparation Time: 10 min.
Cooking Time: 5 min.
Mode of Cooking: Pan Frying
Servings: 2

Ingredients:

- 4 egg whites
- 1 medium zucchini, thinly sliced
- 1 medium tomato, chopped
- 4 fresh basil leaves, chopped
- Salt and pepper to taste
- 2 tsp olive oil

Directions:

1. Heat olive oil in a non-stick skillet over medium heat
2. Add zucchini slices and cook until tender
3. Add tomatoes and cook for an additional minute
4. In a bowl, whisk egg whites with salt and pepper
5. Pour egg whites over the vegetables in the skillet
6. Cook until eggs are set, then fold the omelette in half
7. Garnish with fresh basil

Tips:

- This omelette pairs wonderfully with whole wheat toast for added fiber
- Avoid overcooking the vegetables to maintain nutritional integrity

Nutritional Values: Calories: 140, Fat: 5g, Carbs: 6g, Protein: 18g, Sugar: 4g, Sodium: 300 mg, Potassium: 550 mg, Cholesterol: 0 mg

BELL PEPPER AND ONION MINI QUICHES

Preparation Time: 20 min.
Cooking Time: 25 min.
Mode of Cooking: Baking
Servings: 6
Ingredients:

- 6 egg whites
- 1 red bell pepper, diced
- 1 green bell pepper, diced
- 1 onion, diced
- 1 tsp olive oil
- ½ cup fat-free milk
- Salt and pepper to taste
- ½ tsp dried oregano

- ¼ cup finely chopped parsley

Directions:

1. Preheat oven to 350°F (175°C)
2. Sauté bell peppers and onion in olive oil until soft
3. In a mixing bowl, whisk together egg whites, fat-free milk, salt, pepper, and oregano
4. Stir in the cooked vegetables and parsley
5. Pour mixture into greased muffin tins, filling each about two-thirds full
6. Bake for 25 min. or until the tops are lightly golden and the quiches are set

Tips:

- Mini quiches can be a great on-the-go breakfast option
- Store in an airtight container for up to 4 days in the refrigerator

Nutritional Values: Calories: 90, Fat: 2g, Carbs: 4g, Protein: 12g, Sugar: 3g, Sodium: 220 mg, Potassium: 200 mg, Cholesterol: 0 mg

CAULIFLOWER AND KALE EGG MUFFINS

Preparation Time: 15 min.
Cooking Time: 30 min.
Mode of Cooking: Baking
Servings: 12
Ingredients:

- 8 egg whites
- 2 cups riced cauliflower
- 1 cup chopped kale
- 1/4 cup diced red onion
- 1/2 tsp salt
- 1/4 tsp black pepper
- 1/4 cup low-fat milk

Directions:

1. Preheat oven to 375°F (190°C)
2. Steam cauliflower until tender, about 5 min.
3. Combine steamed cauliflower, chopped kale, and diced onion in a bowl
4. In another bowl, whisk together egg whites, low-fat milk, salt, and pepper
5. Add the vegetable mixture to the egg mixture and stir to combine

6. Spoon into greased muffin cups, filling each about three-quarters full
7. Bake for 30 min. or until muffins are firm and tops are lightly golden

Tips:

- Perfect for meal-prepping for the week
- Can be served with a dollop of low-fat yogurt for added creaminess

Nutritional Values: Calories: 70, Fat: 1g, Carbs: 5g, Protein: 9g, Sugar: 2g, Sodium: 200 mg, Potassium: 250 mg, Cholesterol: 0 mg

HERBED MUSHROOM AND SPINACH FRITTATA

Preparation Time: 10 min.
Cooking Time: 15 min.
Mode of Cooking: Baking
Servings: 4
Ingredients:

- 4 large eggs
- 1 cup fresh spinach, chopped
- 1/2 cup mushrooms, thinly sliced
- 1/4 cup onions, diced
- 1/4 cup low-fat milk
- 1 Tbsp olive oil
- 1/2 tsp dried basil
- 1/2 tsp dried thyme
- salt and pepper to taste

Directions:

1. Preheat oven to 375°F (190°C)
2. In a skillet, heat olive oil over medium heat and sauté onions and mushrooms until soft
3. Add spinach and cook until wilted
4. In a bowl, whisk together eggs, milk, basil, thyme, salt, and pepper
5. Combine the egg mixture with the sautéed vegetables
6. Pour into a greased baking dish and bake for 15 min. or until the eggs are set

Tips:

- Serve with a slice of whole-grain toast for added fiber
- Perfect for making ahead and reheating for a quick breakfast or lunch

Nutritional Values: Calories: 140, Fat: 9g, Carbs: 6g, Protein: 10g, Sugar: 2g, Sodium: 150 mg, Potassium: 220 mg, Cholesterol: 185 mg

SMOKED SALMON AND DILL SCRAMBLE

Preparation Time: 5 min.
Cooking Time: 8 min.
Mode of Cooking: Stovetop
Servings: 2
Ingredients:

- 4 large eggs
- 2 oz. smoked salmon, chopped
- 1 Tbsp fresh dill, chopped
- 1/4 cup low-fat cream cheese
- 2 tsp olive oil
- black pepper to taste

Directions:

1. Heat olive oil in a non-stick pan over medium heat
2. Whisk the eggs in a bowl, then pour into the pan, stirring gently
3. As eggs begin to set, add smoked salmon and cream cheese
4. Cook until eggs are creamy and just set
5. Sprinkle with fresh dill and black pepper before serving

Tips:

- High in omega-3 fatty acids from salmon
- Cream cheese can be replaced with Greek yogurt for a tangier, lower-fat option

Nutritional Values: Calories: 210, Fat: 14g, Carbs: 3g, Protein: 18g, Sugar: 2g, Sodium: 400 mg, Potassium: 200 mg, Cholesterol: 372 mg

TOMATO BASIL OMELETTE

Preparation Time: 5 min.
Cooking Time: 7 min.
Mode of Cooking: Stovetop
Servings: 1
Ingredients:

- 2 large eggs
- 1/2 cup cherry tomatoes, halved
- 1 Tbsp fresh basil, chopped
- 1/4 cup feta cheese, crumbled
- 1 tsp olive oil
- salt and pepper to taste

Directions:

1. Heat oil in a skillet over medium heat
2. Beat the eggs in a bowl and pour into the skillet
3. As the eggs set around the edges, lift them slightly to allow uncooked egg to flow underneath
4. Add tomatoes, feta, and basil on one half
5. Fold omelette over the filling
6. Cook until eggs are fully set and cheese is slightly melted

Tips:

- Consider adding a side of mixed greens for a refreshing breakfast
- Using feta adds flavor while keeping the fat content lower than other cheeses

Nutritional Values: Calories: 180, Fat: 12g, Carbs: 5g, Protein: 12g, Sugar: 3g, Sodium: 310 mg, Potassium: 210 mg, Cholesterol: 370 mg

CHAPTER 7: LUNCH RECIPES

Transitioning into the afternoon, lunch becomes not just a meal but an essential pause, a moment to recharge in the rush of your day—especially critical when your body is adapting to life without a gallbladder. Understanding that midday meals can often be a challenge for those managing digestive sensitivities, the recipes in this chapter are crafted with care to be light on your system while offering comforting, satisfying flavors that convert a simple lunch into a culinary sanctuary.

Invent your personal retreat with salads dressed in homemade, low-fat vinaigrettes that entice the palette without straining digestion. The crunch of fresh greens mingled with an array of colorful vegetables offers a visually appealing and nutrient-rich escape from the mundane. Or perhaps wrap your hands around a delicately assembled sandwich or wrap, with gluten-free bread enveloping tender, lean cuts of meat and a spread of gentle, creamy avocado.

Each recipe is a balance of innovation and simplicity, acknowledging your need for quick, easy-to-prepare dishes that support a busy lifestyle without compromising your dietary requirements. They offer a meditative mix of textures and nuances—from the refreshing crispness of a leafy salad to the soothing, hearty warmth of a light soup—each dish is both a salve and a delight, designed to make lunch a meal to look forward to.

Imagine, for a moment, taking that first bite of a vibrant, healthful salad or savor – each ingredient not only chosen for its flavor but for its ability to aid your digestion and enhance your overall health. Whether at a sunlit table at your workplace or at a quiet kitchen nook at home, these recipes transform your lunchtime into a healing interval, a time that refuels not only your body but also your spirit.

Thus, let each lunch recipe guide you gently through your day, providing the nourishment and comfort you need to continue until evening, making each meal not merely an act of eating but an act of well-being and joy.

7.1 SALADS AND DRESSINGS

KALE AND APPLE SALAD WITH LEMON DRESSING

Preparation Time: 15 min
Cooking Time: none
Mode of Cooking: No Cooking
Servings: 4

Ingredients:

- 1 bunch kale, ribs removed and leaves thinly sliced
- 2 apples, cored and thinly sliced
- 1/4 cup dried cranberries
- 1/4 cup sliced almonds, toasted
- 3 Tbsp olive oil
- 2 Tbsp lemon juice
- 1 tsp honey
- Salt and pepper to taste

Directions:

1. Massage kale with 1 Tbsp olive oil until leaves are tender and bright green
2. Add apples, cranberries, and almonds to kale
3. In a small bowl, whisk together remaining 2 Tbsp olive oil, lemon juice, honey, salt, and pepper to make dressing
4. Pour dressing over salad and toss to coat

Tips:

- Use a mandoline for uniformly thin apple slices for a better texture and distribution throughout the salad
- Add crumbled feta or goat cheese for a touch of creaminess without much fat

Nutritional Values: Calories: 210, Fat: 14g, Carbs: 22g, Protein: 4g, Sugar: 14g, Sodium: 30 mg, Potassium: 397 mg, Cholesterol: 0 mg

SPINACH QUINOA SALAD WITH POMEGRANATE SEEDS

Preparation Time: 20 min
Cooking Time: 15 min
Mode of Cooking: Boiling
Servings: 4
Ingredients:

- 1 cup quinoa
- 2 cups water
- 4 cups baby spinach leaves
- 1/2 cup pomegranate seeds
- 1/4 cup pine nuts, toasted
- 3 Tbsp balsamic vinegar
- 1 Tbsp honey
- 2 Tbsp olive oil
- Salt and pepper to taste

Directions:

1. Rinse quinoa under cold water
2. Cook quinoa in boiling water until it's fluffy and water is absorbed, about 15 min
3. Let quinoa cool
4. In a large bowl, combine cooled quinoa, spinach, pomegranate seeds, and pine nuts
5. In a small bowl, mix balsamic vinegar, honey, olive oil, salt, and pepper to make the dressing
6. Pour dressing over the salad and toss gently to combine

Tips:

- Toast pine nuts lightly to enhance their flavor and add a delightful crunch
- Spinach is rich in vitamins and makes an excellent base for a nutritious salad

Nutritional Values: Calories: 295, Fat: 15g, Carbs: 36g, Protein: 8g, Sugar: 10g, Sodium: 50 mg, Potassium: 512 mg, Cholesterol: 0 mg

BEET AND CARROT SLAW WITH CITRUS VINAIGRETTE

Preparation Time: 10 min
Cooking Time: none
Mode of Cooking: No Cooking
Servings: 4
Ingredients:

- 3 medium beets, peeled and julienned
- 2 large carrots, peeled and julienned
- 1/4 cup chopped cilantro
- 3 Tbsp orange juice
- 2 Tbsp lemon juice
- 1 Tbsp olive oil
- 1 tsp honey
- Salt and pepper to taste

Directions:

1. Combine julienned beets, carrots, and chopped cilantro in a large bowl
2. In a separate small bowl, whisk together orange juice, lemon juice, olive oil, honey, salt, and pepper to create the dressing
3. Pour the dressing over the vegetables and toss well to coat

Tips:

- Use a food processor with a shredding attachment to quickly julienne beets and carrots
- Cilantro not only adds a fresh flavor but also aids in digestion

Nutritional Values: Calories: 123, Fat: 4g, Carbs: 21g, Protein: 2g, Sugar: 16g, Sodium: 76 mg, Potassium: 460 mg, Cholesterol: 0 mg

TARRAGON CHICKEN SALAD WITH GRAPES

Preparation Time: 15 min
Cooking Time: none
Mode of Cooking: No Cooking
Servings: 4
Ingredients:

- 2 cups cooked chicken breast, shredded

- 1 cup red seedless grapes, halved
- 1/4 cup celery, finely chopped
- 1/4 cup low-fat Greek yogurt
- 1 Tbsp fresh tarragon, chopped
- 1 Tbsp lemon juice
- 1 tsp Dijon mustard
- Salt and pepper to taste

Directions:

1. Combine shredded chicken, grapes, and celery in a large bowl
2. In a separate small bowl, whisk together Greek yogurt, tarragon, lemon juice, and Dijon mustard until smooth
3. Pour dressing over chicken mixture and toss to coat evenly
4. Season with salt and pepper
5. Chill in the refrigerator before serving

Tips:

- Opt for organic chicken to avoid added hormones and chemicals
- Tarr.The salad can be stored in the refrigerator for up to two days, enhancing flavors

Nutritional Values: Calories: 165, Fat: 3g, Carbs: 10g, Protein: 24g, Sugar: 7g, Sodium: 190 mg, Potassium: 270 mg, Cholesterol: 50 mg

LEMON HERB QUINOA & CHICKPEA SALAD

Preparation Time: 20 min
Cooking Time: none
Mode of Cooking: No Cooking
Servings: 6
Ingredients:

- 1 cup quinoa, cooked and cooled
- 1 can (15 oz) chickpeas, rinsed and drained
- 1/2 cucumber, diced
- 1/2 red bell pepper, diced
- 1/4 cup fresh parsley, finely chopped
- 1/4 cup fresh mint, finely chopped
- 3 Tbsp lemon juice
- 2 Tbsp olive oil
- Salt and pepper to taste

Directions:

1. In a large mixing bowl, combine cooked quinoa, chickpeas, cucumber, and red bell pepper
2. Add chopped parsley and mint
3. In a small bowl, whisk together lemon juice, olive oil, salt, and pepper to make the dressing
4. Pour the dressing over the salad and toss gently to mix well
5. Refrigerate for an hour before serving to allow flavors to meld

Tips:

- Use extra virgin olive oil for added antioxidant benefits
- Lemon juice not only flavors the salad but also aids in iron absorption from the chickpeas

Nutritional Values: Calories: 210, Fat: 8g, Carbs: 28g, Protein: 8g, Sugar: 3g, Sodium: 300 mg, Potassium: 350 mg, Cholesterol: 0 mg

ASIAN TOFU AND EDAMAME SALAD

Preparation Time: 10 min
Cooking Time: none
Mode of Cooking: No Cooking
Servings: 4
Ingredients:

- 1 block (14 oz) firm tofu, drained and cubed
- 1 cup edamame, shelled and cooked
- 1 carrot, julienned
- 1/2 cup red cabbage, shredded
- 2 Tbsp soy sauce, low sodium
- 1 Tbsp sesame oil
- 1 tsp ginger, grated
- 1 tsp garlic, minced
- 1 Tbsp cilantro, chopped
- Sesame seeds for garnish

Directions:

1. Combine tofu, edamame, carrot, and red cabbage in a large salad bowl
2. In a small mixing bowl, whisk together soy sauce, sesame oil, ginger, and garlic to create the dressing

3. Pour the dressing over the salad and toss to coat thoroughly

4. Garnish with chopped cilantro and sesame seeds

Tips:

• Prefer organic soy products to reduce exposure to pesticides

• Sesame oil and seeds add a burst of flavor and are excellent sources of calcium

Nutritional Values: Calories: 190, Fat: 12g, Carbs: 10g, Protein: 12g, Sugar: 3g, Sodium: 330 mg, Potassium: 400 mg, Cholesterol: 0 mg

CITRUS POPPYSEED DRESSING

Preparation Time: 5 min

Cooking Time: none

Mode of Cooking: No Cooking

Servings: 8

Ingredients:

• ¼ cup fresh orange juice
• 2 Tbsp fresh lemon juice
• 1 Tbsp honey
• 1 tsp Dijon mustard
• 1 Tbsp poppy seeds
• ¼ cup white wine vinegar
• 2 Tbsp olive oil
• Salt to taste

Directions:

1. Combine orange juice, lemon juice, honey, and Dijon mustard in a large bowl

2. Whisk in white wine vinegar and olive oil until the mixture is emulsified

3. Stir in poppy seeds and salt to taste

Tips:

• Use a fine mesh strainer to ensure smoothness of the citrus juices for a clearer dressing

• Store in an airtight container in the refrigerator for up to 5 days

• Shake well before each use

Nutritional Values: Calories: 45, Fat: 3.5g, Carbs: 4g, Protein: 0.1g, Sugar: 3.6g, Sodium: 12 mg, Potassium: 13 mg, Cholesterol: 0 mg

HERBAL VINAIGRETTE

Preparation Time: 10 min

Cooking Time: none

Mode of Cooking: No Cooking

Servings: 8

Ingredients:

• 3 Tbsp apple cider vinegar
• 1 tsp fresh garlic, minced
• 1 Tbsp fresh basil leaves, finely chopped
• 1 Tbsp fresh parsley, finely chopped
• ½ tsp dried oregano
• ¼ cup olive oil
• Salt and pepper to taste

Directions:

1. Combine apple cider vinegar and minced garlic in a bowl

2. Add finely chopped basil, parsley, and dried oregano

3. Gradually whisk in olive oil to create an emulsion

4. Season with salt and pepper

Tips:

• Ensure herbs are finely chopped to release more flavors

• Can be stored in an airtight container in the fridge for up to a week

• Perfect as a marinade for lean proteins or drizzled over grilled vegetables

Nutritional Values: Calories: 62, Fat: 6.7g, Carbs: 0.4g, Protein: 0.1g, Sugar: 0.1g, Sodium: 2 mg, Potassium: 11 mg, Cholesterol: 0 mg

GINGER LIME DRESSING

Preparation Time: 5 min

Cooking Time: none

Mode of Cooking: No Cooking

Servings: 6

Ingredients:

• Juice of 2 limes
• 1 Tbsp ginger, grated
• 2 tsp soy sauce, low sodium
• 1 Tbsp honey
• ¼ cup olive oil

- Pinch of black pepper

Directions:

1. Combine lime juice and grated ginger in a small bowl
2. Add low sodium soy sauce and honey and mix well
3. Gradually whisk in olive oil and season with a pinch of black pepper

Tips:

- Grate the ginger finely to extract more juice and flavor
- Use fresh lime juice for the best flavor
- Good pairing for cabbage slaws or cold noodle salads

Nutritional Values: Calories: 70, Fat: 7g, Carbs: 3g, Protein: 0.1g, Sugar: 2.5g, Sodium: 120 mg, Potassium: 8 mg, Cholesterol: 0 mg

7.2 SANDWICHES AND WRAPS

CURRIED TURKEY AND AVOCADO WRAP WITH WHOLE WHEAT TORTILLA

Preparation Time: 15 min
Cooking Time: none
Mode of Cooking: No Cooking
Servings: 2
Ingredients:

- 1 large whole wheat tortilla
- 4 oz. turkey breast, thinly sliced
- 1 ripe avocado, mashed
- 1 small carrot, grated
- ¼ cup cucumber, thinly sliced
- 1 Tbsp low-fat Greek yogurt
- ½ tsp curry powder
- Salt to taste
- Fresh cilantro leaves, chopped

Directions:

1. Spread the mashed avocado onto the whole wheat tortilla
2. Layer the turkey slices, grated carrot, and cucumber slices on top of the avocado

3. In a small bowl, mix the Greek yogurt with curry powder and salt, then drizzle over the turkey and vegetables
4. Sprinkle chopped cilantro leaves over the contents
5. Carefully roll the tortilla, ensuring the fillings stay inside, and cut into halves

Tips:

- Choose a ripe avocado for easier mashing and richer flavor
- Adding lemon juice to avocado prevents browning and adds a fresh zest

Nutritional Values: Calories: 320, Fat: 15g, Carbs: 27g, Protein: 22g, Sugar: 2g, Sodium: 600 mg, Potassium: 560 mg, Cholesterol: 30 mg

SMOKED SALMON AND CUCUMBER WHOLEGRAIN BAGEL

Preparation Time: 10 min
Cooking Time: none
Mode of Cooking: No Cooking
Servings: 1
Ingredients:

- 1 whole grain bagel, halved
- 2 oz. smoked salmon
- 2 Tbsp low-fat cream cheese
- ¼ cup arugula
- 4 thin slices of cucumber
- 1 tsp capers
- 1 Tbsp red onion, finely chopped
- Fresh dill for garnish

Directions:

1. Toast the whole grain bagel to desired crispness
2. Spread each half with low-fat cream cheese ♧ Top one side with smoked salmon, cucumber slices, and arugula
3. Sprinkle capers and chopped red onion over the salmon
4. Garnish with fresh dill, then close the bagel with the other half

Tips:

- To enhance flavor, allow the cream cheese to reach room temperature before spreading
- Pressing the bagel down after assembly helps to distribute flavors evenly

Nutritional Values: Calories: 300, Fat: 9g, Carbs: 38g, Protein: 19g, Sugar: 6g, Sodium: 820 mg, Potassium: 280 mg, Cholesterol: 20 mg

CHICKPEA HUMMUS AND VEGGIE LAVASH WRAP

Preparation Time: 20 min
Cooking Time: none
Mode of Cooking: No Cooking
Servings: 2
Ingredients:

- 1 cup cooked chickpeas
- 1 Tbsp tahini
- 1 garlic clove, minced
- 2 Tbsp lemon juice
- Salt and pepper to taste
- 1 large piece of Lavash bread
- ½ red bell pepper, thinly sliced
- ½ cucumber, thinly sliced
- ¼ cup shredded carrots
- ¼ cup mixed greens

Directions:

1. In a food processor, blend chickpeas, tahini, garlic, lemon juice, salt, and pepper until smooth to make hummus
2. Spread the hummus evenly over the Lavash bread
3. Layer red bell pepper, cucumber, shredded carrots, and mixed greens on top of the hummus
4. Roll up the lavash tightly, slice into portions

Tips:

- Using homemade hummus ensures control over the texture and fat content
- Adding lemon zest to the humus can brighten the flavor profile

Nutritional Values: Calories: 270, Fat: 9g, Carbs: 42g, Protein: 12g, Sugar: 5g, Sodium: 470 mg, Potassium: 390 mg, Cholesterol: 0 mg

TURKEY AVOCADO WRAP

Preparation Time: 15 min
Cooking Time: none
Mode of Cooking: No Cooking
Servings: 2
Ingredients:

- 8 oz. lean turkey breast, thinly sliced
- 2 whole grain tortillas
- 1 ripe avocado, mashed
- 1 cup fresh spinach leaves
- 1 small cucumber, thinly sliced
- 2 Tbsp low-fat Greek yogurt
- 1 tsp lemon juice
- Salt and pepper to taste

Directions:

1. Spread the mashed avocado evenly on each tortilla
2. Add a layer of turkey slices over the avocado
3. Mix Greek yogurt with lemon juice, salt, and pepper then drizzle over the turkey
4. Top with spinach leaves and cucumber slices
5. Roll up the tortillas tightly, slice in half, and serve

Tips:

- Opt for salt-free seasonings to enhance flavor without adding sodium
- Prepare the night before for a grab-and-go lunch option

Nutritional Values: Calories: 320, Fat: 9g, Carbs: 32g, Protein: 26g, Sugar: 3g, Sodium: 210 mg, Potassium: 690 mg, Cholesterol: 50 mg

GRILLED CHICKEN HUMMUS WRAP

Preparation Time: 20 min
Cooking Time: 10 min
Mode of Cooking: Grilling
Servings: 4
Ingredients:

- 16 oz. chicken breast, boneless, skinless

- 4 whole grain tortillas
- 1 cup hummus, low-fat
- 1 red bell pepper, deseeded and thinly sliced
- 1 carrot, julienned
- 1 Tbsp olive oil
- Salt and black pepper to taste

Directions:

1. Season chicken breasts with salt and pepper, brush with a bit of olive oil
2. Grill chicken over medium heat until fully cooked and juices run clear, approximately 5 to 6 min per side
3. Let chicken rest for a few minutes then slice thinly
4. Spread hummus on tortillas
5. Layer grilled chicken, bell pepper, and carrot slices on top of the hummus
6. Roll up the tortillas tightly and slice in half

Tips:

- Using hummus instead of mayonnaise provides flavor and creaminess without excess fat
- Keep wraps refrigerated until serving to maintain freshness

Nutritional Values: Calories: 295, Fat: 9g, Carbs: 28g, Protein: 24g, Sugar: 4g, Sodium: 310 mg, Potassium: 460 mg, Cholesterol: 60 mg

BEEF AND MUSTARD GREENS WRAP

Preparation Time: 15 min
Cooking Time: none
Mode of Cooking: No Cooking
Servings: 2
Ingredients:

- 8 oz. roast beef, thinly sliced
- 2 whole grain tortillas
- 1 cup mustard greens, chopped
- 1/4 cup red onion, thinly sliced
- 2 radishes, thinly sliced
- 2 Tbsp low-fat Caesar dressing
- Salt and pepper to taste

Directions:

1. Lay out the tortillas on a flat surface

2. Distribute the roast beef slices evenly over the tortillas
3. Top the beef with mustard greens, red onion, and radishes
4. Drizzle with low-fat Caesar dressing and season with salt and pepper
5. Roll the tortillas tightly, slice in half, and serve

Tips:

- Substitute traditional heavy dressings with low-fat Caesar for flavor without the fat
- Mustard greens add a peppery kick that complements the roast beef

Nutritional Values: Calories: 275, Fat: 8g, Carbs: 25g, Protein: 25g, Sugar: 2g, Sodium: 410 mg, Potassium: 480 mg, Cholesterol: 45 mg

MEDITERRANEAN HUMMUS VEGGIE WRAP

Preparation Time: 15 min
Cooking Time: none
Mode of Cooking: No Cooking
Servings: 2
Ingredients:

- 1 large whole grain tortilla
- ¼ cup hummus
- ½ cup spinach, fresh
- ¼ cup cucumber, sliced thin
- ¼ cup bell pepper, julienned
- 2 Tbsp feta cheese, crumbled
- 2 Tbsp olives, sliced
- 1 Tbsp red onion, finely chopped
- 1 tsp olive oil
- 1 tsp lemon juice
- ½ tsp dried oregano

Directions:

1. Spread hummus evenly across the tortilla
2. Lay spinach leaves on top
3. Add cucumber, bell pepper, feta cheese, olives, and red onion evenly over the spinach
4. Drizzle with olive oil and lemon juice, then sprinkle oregano
5. Roll the tortilla tightly, slice in half diagonally

Tips:

- Opt for low-fat or fat-free feta to minimize fat content
- Add a sprinkle of chili flakes for a mild spicy kick if desired
- Wrap can be made a few hours ahead and kept refrigerated until serving

Nutritional Values: Calories: 295, Fat: 15g, Carbs: 32g, Protein: 9g, Sugar: 3g, Sodium: 580 mg, Potassium: 210 mg, Cholesterol: 8 mg

CARROT AND AVOCADO CALIFORNIA WRAP

Preparation Time: 20 min
Cooking Time: none
Mode of Cooking: No Cooking
Servings: 2
Ingredients:

- 1 large whole grain tortilla
- ¼ cup mashed avocado
- ½ cup mixed greens
- ½ carrot, julienne
- ¼ cup alfalfa sprouts
- 2 Tbsp pumpkin seeds
- ¼ tsp garlic powder
- ¼ tsp black pepper
- 1 Tbsp lime juice
- 1 Tbsp cilantro, chopped

Directions:

1. Spread mashed avocado on the tortilla
2. Season with garlic powder, black pepper, and lime juice
3. Add mixed greens, julienne carrots, alfalfa sprouts, and chopped cilantro
4. Sprinkle with pumpkin seeds
5. Roll the tortilla tightly, then slice in half

Tips:

- Use ripe avocados for easier mashing and a creamier texture
- Carrots can be pre-julienned to save on prep time
- Pumpkin seeds can be toasted for extra flavor

Nutritional Values: Calories: 265, Fat: 14g, Carbs: 29g, Protein: 7g, Sugar: 4g, Sodium: 180 mg, Potassium: 495 mg, Cholesterol: 0 mg

SPICY TOFU LETTUCE WRAP

Preparation Time: 10 min
Cooking Time: 5 min
Mode of Cooking: Pan Frying
Servings: 2
Ingredients:

- ½ block firm tofu, crumbled
- 2 large leaves of Romaine lettuce
- 1 Tbsp olive oil
- 1's green onions, chopped
- 1 tsp soy sauce, low sodium
- ½ tsp chili powder
- ½ tsp cumin powder
- ¼ cup red bell pepper, diced
- 1 Tbsp lime juice

Directions:

1. Heat olive oil in a non-stick pan, add crumbled tofu and pan-fry until golden
2. Add chili and cumin powder, stir well
3. Mix in soy sauce and lime juice
4. Cook for another minute
5. Remove from heat and assemble in lettuce leaves with diced red bell pepper and green onions

Tips:

- Chili can be adjusted as per tolerance level
- Use iceberg lettuce for a crunchier texture as an alternative
- Serve immediately after cooking to enjoy the crispness of the lettuce

Nutritional Values: Calories: 230, Fat: 11g, Carbs: 18g, Protein: 16g, Sugar: 3g, Sodium: 330 mg, Potassium: 300 mg, Cholesterol: 0 mg

7.3 Light Soups and Broths

Ginger Turmeric Chicken Broth

Preparation Time: 10 min
Cooking Time: 1 hr
Mode of Cooking: Simmering
Servings: 4
Ingredients:

- 2 lb. of chicken bones
- 8 C. of water
- 1 medium onion, quartered
- 2 carrots, chopped
- 2 celery stalks, chopped
- 4 slices of fresh ginger
- 2 cloves of garlic, peeled
- 1 Tbsp of ground turmeric
- 1 tsp of black peppercorns
- 1 bay leaf

Directions:

1. Place all ingredients in a large pot and bring to a boil
2. Reduce heat to a simmer and partially cover
3. Simmer for 1 hr, skimming foam as needed
4. Strain through a fine mesh sieve and discard solids

Tips:
- Drink warm to soothe digestion
- Add salt to taste before serving if desired
- Store in the refrigerator for up to 5 days or freeze for longer storage

Nutritional Values: Calories: 40, Fat: 1g, Carbs: 3g, Protein: 5g, Sugar: 1g, Sodium: 95 mg, Potassium: 150 mg, Cholesterol: 15 mg

Fennel and Leek Vegetable Broth

Preparation Time: 15 min
Cooking Time: 45 min
Mode of Cooking: Simmering
Servings: 4
Ingredients:

- 1 fennel bulb, chopped
- 2 leeks, white and light green parts only, cleaned and sliced
- 1 carrot, peeled and sliced
- 1 celery stalk, sliced
- 6 C. vegetable stock
- 1 tsp dried thyme
- 1 bay leaf
- Juice of 1 lemon
- Fresh parsley, finely chopped for garnish

Directions:

1. Combine fennel, leeks, carrot, and celery in a large pot
2. Add vegetable stock, thyme, and bay leaf
3. Bring to a boil, then reduce heat and simmer for 45 min
4. Remove from heat and stir in lemon juice
5. Strain the broth, garnish with parsley

Tips:
- Serve with a sprinkle of freshly cracked black pepper to enhance flavor
- Can be consumed alone or used as a base for other soup recipes
- Keeps well in the fridge for up to 4 days

Nutritional Values: Calories: 35, Fat: 0g, Carbs: 8g, Protein: 1g, Sugar: 3g, Sodium: 800 mg, Potassium: 180 mg, Cholesterol: 0 mg

Miso Mushroom Broth

Preparation Time: 20 min
Cooking Time: 30 min
Mode of Cooking: Simmering
Servings: 2
Ingredients:

- 4 C. water
- 1 C. shiitake mushrooms, thinly sliced
- 2 tsp miso paste
- 1 small onion, sliced
- 1 clove of garlic, minced
- 1 tsp grated ginger
- 1 Tbsp tamari sauce
- 1 Tbsp olive oil
- Fresh chives, chopped for garnish

Directions:

1. Heat olive oil in a pot over medium heat

2. Sauté onion, garlic, and ginger until onion is translucent
3. Add water and bring to a simmer
4. Add mushrooms and simmer for 20 min
5. Remove from heat, stir in miso paste and tamari sauce
6. Strain broth, garnish with chives

Tips:
- Do not boil after adding miso to preserve beneficial probiotics
- Use different types of mushrooms for varying flavors and textures
- Ideal for a soothing evening meal

Nutritional Values: Calories: 58, Fat: 3g, Carbs: 6g, Protein: 2g, Sugar: 2g, Sodium: 740 mg, Potassium: 220 mg, Cholesterol: 0 mg

SILKEN TOFU AND MUSHROOM SOUP

Preparation Time: 15 min.
Cooking Time: 25 min.
Mode of Cooking: Stovetop
Servings: 4
Ingredients:
- 1 Tbsp olive oil
- 2 cups shiitake mushrooms, thinly sliced
- 1 block silken tofu, cubed
- 4 cups vegetable broth
- 1 Tbsp soy sauce
- 1 tsp grated ginger
- 1 garlic clove, minced
- 2 green onions, chopped
- 1 tsp sesame oil
- Salt and pepper to taste

Directions:
1. Heat olive oil in a large pot over medium heat
2. Add sliced mushrooms, cook until soft, about 5 minutes
3. Add minced garlic and grated ginger, cook for another 2 minutes
4. Pour in vegetable broth, soy sauce, and bring to a simmer

5. Gently add cubed silken tofu to the pot, let simmer for 15 minutes without boiling to avoid breaking the tofu
6. Stir in sesame oil, and season with salt and pepper
7. Garnish with chopped green onions before serving

Tips:
- Stir gently to keep tofu from breaking
- Add a dash of chili oil for a slight kick without making it too spicy

Nutritional Values: Calories: 105, Fat: 5g, Carbs: 8g, Protein: 6g, Sugar: 2g, Sodium: 460 mg, Potassium: 215 mg, Cholesterol: 0 mg

CAULIFLOWER LEEK SOUP WITH NUTRITIONAL YEAST

Preparation Time: 10 min.
Cooking Time: 30 min.
Mode of Cooking: Stovetop
Servings: 6
Ingredients:
- 1 Tbsp coconut oil
- 1 large leek, white and light green parts only, finely chopped
- 1 medium head cauliflower, broken into florets
- 5 cups low-sodium vegetable stock
- 1/4 cup nutritional yeast
- 1 tsp dried thyme
- Salt and pepper to taste

Directions:
1. Melt coconut oil in a pot over medium heat
2. Add chopped leeks and sauté until translucent, about 7 minutes
3. Add cauliflower florets and stir for a couple of minutes
4. Pour in vegetable stock and bring to a boil
5. Reduce heat and simmer until cauliflower is tender, about 20 minutes
6. Stir in nutritional yeast and dried thyme
7. Puree with an immersion blender until smooth
8. Season with salt and pepper to taste

Tips:
- Serve with a sprinkle of paprika for a color pop
- Ideal paired with a fresh green salad

Nutritional Values: Calories: 98, Fat: 3g, Carbs: 14g, Protein: 6g, Sugar: 4g, Sodium: 300 mg, Potassium: 430 mg, Cholesterol: 0 mg

CARROT GINGER SOUP WITH APPLE

Preparation Time: 20 min.
Cooking Time: 40 min.
Mode of Cooking: Stovetop
Servings: 4
Ingredients:
- 2 Tbsp olive oil
- 5 large carrots, peeled and chopped
- 1 apple, peeled, cored, and chopped
- 1 small onion, chopped
- 2 Tbsp fresh ginger, minced
- 4 cups low-sodium vegetable broth
- 1 tsp lemon juice
- Salt and pepper to taste

Directions:

1. Heat olive oil in a large saucepan over medium heat
2. Add chopped onion and ginger, cook until onion is translucent, about 5 minutes
3. Add chopped carrots and apple, cook for another 5 minutes
4. Pour in vegetable broth and bring to a boil
5. Reduce heat to low and simmer until carrots and apple are soft, about 30 minutes
6. Puree the mixture until smooth using an immersion blender
7. Stir in lemon juice, season with salt and pepper
8. Serve hot

Tips:
- Add a spoonful of low-fat Greek yogurt for creaminess without the fat
- Garnish with fresh parsley for an extra touch of freshness

Nutritional Values: Calories: 140, Fat: 5g, Carbs: 24g, Protein: 2g, Sugar: 12g, Sodium: 280 mg, Potassium: 370 mg, Cholesterol: 0 mg

TURKEY AND VEGETABLE MEDLEY SOUP

Preparation Time: 15 min
Cooking Time: 35 min
Mode of Cooking: Simmering
Servings: 4
Ingredients:
- 200g ground turkey, lean
- 1 cup carrots, diced
- 1 cup zucchini, diced
- 1 cup celery, diced
- 3 cloves garlic, minced
- 1 liter chicken broth, low-sodium
- 1 tsp thyme, dried
- ½ tsp parsley, dried
- Salt to taste
- Pepper to taste

Directions:

1. Sauté garlic and turkey in a large pot until turkey is browned
2. Add carrots, celery, and zucchini and cook for 5 minutes
3. Pour in chicken broth and bring to a boil
4. Reduce heat and simmer for 30 minutes
5. Season with thyme, parsley, salt, and pepper

Tips:
- Opt for lean turkey to reduce fat content
- Stir occasionally to prevent sticking
- Serve hot for best flavor

Nutritional Values: Calories: 150, Fat: 3g, Carbs: 10g, Protein: 20g, Sugar: 5g, Sodium: 300 mg, Potassium: 350 mg, Cholesterol: 30 mg

CHICKEN AND SPINACH BROTH

Preparation Time: 10 min
Cooking Time: 20 min
Mode of Cooking: Boiling
Servings: 4
Ingredients:
- 200g chicken breast, cubed, skinless

- 2 cups spinach, fresh
- 1 onion, chopped
- 2 liters water
- 1 chicken bouillon cube, low-sodium
- 1 tsp olive oil
- Salt to taste
- Pepper to taste

Directions:

1. Heat olive oil in a saucepan and cook onion until translucent
2. Add chicken and cook until no longer pink
   ♨ Add water and bouillon cube and bring to a boil
3. Add spinach, simmer for 15 minutes
4. Season with salt and pepper

Tips:

- Use skinless chicken breast for lower fat content
- Can be pureed for a smoother texture
- Adjust seasoning according to taste

Nutritional Values: Calories: 120, Fat: 2g, Carbs: 3g, Protein: 22g, Sugar: 1g, Sodium: 200 mg, Potassium: 400 mg, Cholesterol: 50 mg

BEEF AND MUSHROOM CLEAR SOUP

Preparation Time: 20 min
Cooking Time: 40 min
Mode of Cooking: Simmering
Servings: 4
Ingredients:

- 150g beef sirloin, thinly sliced
- 1 cup mushrooms, sliced
- 1 carrot, julienne
- 1 liter beef broth, low-fat
- 2 Tbsp soy sauce, low-sodium
- 1 tsp ginger, minced
- 2 scallions, chopped
- Salt to taste
- Pepper to taste

Directions:

1. Brown beef slices in a non-stick pan without oil
2. Remove beef and sauté mushrooms and ginger in the same pan for 5 minutes
3. Add beef, vegetables, and beef broth to the pan
4. Bring to a boil, then simmer for 35 minutes
5. Add soy sauce, scallions, salt, and pepper before serving

Tips:

- Slice beef thinly to ensure quick cooking
- Opt for low-fat broth to keep it digestion-friendly
- Garnish with scallions for an extra flavor boost

Nutritional Values: Calories: 160, Fat: 5g, Carbs: 4g, Protein: 25g, Sugar: 2g, Sodium: 250 mg, Potassium: 500 mg, Cholesterol: 40 mg

CHAPTER 8: DINNER RECIPES

As the day winds down, the importance of a peaceful, nourishing dinner becomes apparent, especially when your body is navigating life without a gallbladder. This evening meal is your opportunity to not only satiate your hunger but also to soothe and prepare your body for rest. The recipes in this chapter are designed to deliver maximum flavor with minimal strain on your digestive system, making each dinner a restorative experience.

Imagine settling into the evening with a dish of tender, lean protein—perhaps a grilled chicken breast or a baked fillet of fish, seasoned perfectly with herbs that not only enhance flavor but are friends to your digestion. Accompany these with sides of hearty vegetables, steamed or roasted to maintain their nutritive value while bringing out their inherent sweetness and texture. Every bite is crafted to support your health and please your palate without overwhelming your system.

For those who enjoy the comforting embrace of starches, low-fat pasta and rice dishes are reimagined in this chapter. Through careful ingredient selection and preparation techniques, these staples are transformed into digestible dishes that complement your nutritional needs. Delicate sauces, rich in flavor yet low in fat, coat the pasta, while herbs and spices infuse the rice, turning these simple grains into exotic escapes that are gentle on your digestive tract.

These dinner recipes are more than just meals; they are a chance to reconnect with the culinary joy that might have been overshadowed by dietary restrictions. Each dish is a celebration of balance and taste, crafted to ensure that your last meal of the day is as comforting as it is nourishing.

With each recipe, envision how dinner can transform from a routine meal into an enjoyable, stress-free culinary journey that nurtures both body and soul. As you embrace these evening meals, allow them to usher you into a night of restful sleep, knowing you have nourished your body with care and consideration.

8.1 LEAN PROTEIN DISHES

GINGER-SOY POACHED COD

Preparation Time: 10 min.
Cooking Time: 15 min.
Mode of Cooking: Poaching
Servings: 4
Ingredients:

- 4 cod fillets, approximately 6 oz. each
- 2 cups low-sodium vegetable broth
- 1/4 cup soy sauce
- 2-inch piece of ginger, peeled and thinly sliced
- 2 cloves garlic, minced
- 4 green onions, chopped
- 1 tsp freshly ground black pepper

Directions:

1. Combine vegetable broth, soy sauce, ginger, garlic, and black pepper in a deep skillet and bring to a simmer
2. Add cod fillets to the skillet, ensuring they are submerged
3. Cover and poach over medium heat until fish flakes easily with a fork, about 12-15 min.
4. Remove cod gently and garnish with green onions

Tips:

- Serve with steamed vegetables for a complete meal

- Avoid overcooking to maintain the delicate texture of the fish

Nutritional Values: Calories: 190, Fat: 2g, Carbs: 2g, Protein: 40g, Sugar: 1g, Sodium: 580 mg, Potassium: 960 mg, Cholesterol: 60 mg

LEMON-THYME BAKED TILAPIA

Preparation Time: 15 min.
Cooking Time: 20 min.
Mode of Cooking: Baking
Servings: 4
Ingredients:

- 4 tilapia fillets, approximately 6 oz. each
- 1 lemon, thinly sliced
- 1 Tbsp fresh thyme leaves
- 1 Tbsp olive oil
- Salt and pepper to taste
- 1/4 cup low-fat chicken broth

Directions:

1. Preheat oven to 375°F (190°C)
2. Arrange tilapia fillets in a baking dish
3. Top each fillet with lemon slices and sprinkle with thyme, salt, and pepper
4. Drizzle olive oil and chicken broth over the fillets
5. Bake uncovered until fish is cooked through and flaky, about 20 min.

Tips:

- Keep the baking dish covered with foil if the fish is browning too quickly
- Pair with a quinoa salad for a fiber-rich side dish

Nutritional Values: Calories: 180, Fat: 5g, Carbs: 3g, Protein: 34g, Sugar: 0g, Sodium: 125 mg, Potassium: 830 mg, Cholesterol: 85 mg

CHILI LIME SHRIMP SKEWERS

Preparation Time: 20 min.
Cooking Time: 8 min.
Mode of Cooking: Grilling
Servings: 4
Ingredients:

- 24 large shrimp, peeled and deveined
- 2 Tbsp lime juice
- 1 tsp chili powder
- 1 clove garlic, minced
- Salt to taste
- 1 Tbsp olive oil
- 8 skewers, soaked in water if wooden

Directions:

1. Preheat grill to medium-high heat
2. In a bowl, mix lime juice, chili The text exceeds the output character limit. This is the reason why the rest of the recipes, instructions, and extra details were not included in this response.

Tips:

-

Nutritional Values:

HERBED TURKEY BREAST WITH ORANGE ZEST

Preparation Time: 15 min.
Cooking Time: 1 hr. 30 min.
Mode of Cooking: Roasting
Servings: 6
Ingredients:

- 3 lb. turkey breast, boneless and skinless
- 2 Tbsp olive oil
- 1 Tbsp fresh rosemary, finely chopped
- 1 Tbsp fresh thyme, finely chopped
- 2 cloves garlic, minced
- Zest of 1 orange
- 1 tsp salt
- 1/2 tsp black pepper
- 1/2 cup low-sodium chicken broth

Directions:

1. Preheat oven to 350°F (175°C)
2. Pat turkey breast dry and make diagonal cuts on the surface
3. In a bowl, combine olive oil, rosemary, thyme, garlic, orange zest, salt, and pepper
4. Rub the mixture thoroughly over and into the cuts of the turkey
5. Place in a roasting pan and pour chicken broth around

6. Roast in the oven until the internal temperature reaches 165°F (74°C), about 90 min.
7. Let rest before slicing

Tips:

● To retain moisture, tent the turkey with foil if it browns too quickly

● For a crisper skin, broil for the last 5 min.

Nutritional Values: Calories: 310, Fat: 12g, Carbs: 3g, Protein: 46g, Sugar: 1g, Sodium: 620 mg, Potassium: 450 mg, Cholesterol: 125 mg

BAKED LEMON AND DILL CHICKEN

Preparation Time: 10 min.
Cooking Time: 25 min.
Mode of Cooking: Baking
Servings: 4
Ingredients:

● 4 chicken breasts, boneless and skinless
● 1 lemon, juiced and zested
● 2 Tbsp dill, freshly chopped
● 1 Tbsp olive oil
● 1/2 tsp garlic powder
● Salt to taste
● Pepper to taste
● 1/4 cup water

Directions:

1. Preheat oven to 375°F (190°C)
2. In a mixing bowl, combine lemon juice and zest, dill, olive oil, garlic powder, salt, and pepper
3. Place chicken breasts in a baking dish and pour the mixture over them
4. Add water to the dish
5. Bake in the preheated oven until chicken is cooked through, about 25 min.

Tips:

● Serve with a side of steamed vegetables to complete this meal

● Use parchment paper in the baking dish for easier cleanup

Nutritional Values: Calories: 195, Fat: 5g, Carbs: 3g, Protein: 35g, Sugar: 0g, Sodium: 220 mg, Potassium: 290 mg, Cholesterol: 85 mg

PAN-SEARED COD WITH PARSLEY GREMOLATA

Preparation Time: 10 min.
Cooking Time: 12 min.
Mode of Cooking: Pan Searing
Servings: 4
Ingredients:

● 4 cod filets, 4 oz. each
● 2 Tbsp olive oil
● 1/4 cup parsley, finely chopped
● 3 cloves garlic, minced
● Zest of 1 lemon
● 1/2 tsp salt
● 1/4 tsp black pepper
● Lemon wedges for serving

Directions:

1. Heat olive oil in a large skillet over medium-high heat
2. Season cod filets with salt and pepper
3. Sear cod for about 6 min on each side or until cooked through
4. In a small bowl, combine parsley, garlic, and lemon zest
5. Sprinkle gremolata over cooked cod before serving

Tips:

● Adding a squeeze of fresh lemon juice enhances the flavors

● Pair with a quinoa salad for a hearty meal

Nutritional Values: Calories: 140, Fat: 5g, Carbs: 1g, Protein: 23g, Sugar: 0g, Sodium: 340 mg, Potassium: 460 mg, Cholesterol: 60 mg

QUINOA AND BLACK BEAN STUFFED PEPPERS

Preparation Time: 20 min
Cooking Time: 35 min
Mode of Cooking: Baking
Servings: 4

Ingredients:

- 2 large red bell peppers, halved and seeds removed
- 1 cup quinoa, rinsed
- 2 cups vegetable broth
- 1 can (15 oz.) black beans, drained and rinsed
- 1 cup corn kernels, fresh or frozen
- 1 small red onion, finely chopped
- 2 cloves garlic, minced
- 1 tsp cumin
- ½ tsp chili powder
- ¼ cup fresh cilantro, chopped
- 1 lime, juiced
- Salt and pepper to taste

Directions:

1. Preheat oven to 375°F (190°C)
2. In a saucepan, combine quinoa with vegetable broth, bring to a boil, reduce to simmer, cover, and cook until all liquid is absorbed, about 15 min
3. In a large bowl, combine cooked quinoa, black beans, corn, onion, garlic, cumin, chili powder, cilantro, lime juice, salt, and pepper
4. Stuff each bell pepper half with the quinoa mixture
5. Place stuffed peppers in a baking dish, cover with foil, and bake in preheated oven for 20 min. Remove foil and bake for an additional 15 min until peppers are tender

Tips:

- Consider adding a sprinkle of low-fat cheese during the last 5 min. of baking for a melty touch
- Serve with a dollop of fat-free Greek yogurt for a creamy texture

Nutritional Values: Calories: 290, Fat: 3g, Carbs: 54g, Protein: 12g, Sugar: 8g, Sodium: 300 mg, Potassium: 770 mg, Cholesterol: 0 mg

LENTIL AND MUSHROOM RAGOUT

Preparation Time: 15 min
Cooking Time: 25 min
Mode of Cooking: Simmering
Servings: 4

Ingredients:

- 1 Tbsp olive oil
- 1 lb. mushrooms, thinly sliced
- 1 cup dried lentils, rinsed
- 3 cups low-sodium vegetable broth
- 1 carrot, peeled and diced
- 1 celery stalk, diced
- 1 onion, diced
- 2 cloves garlic, minced
- 1 tsp dried thyme
- 1 tsp dried rosemary
- 1 bay leaf
- Salt and pepper to taste

Directions:

1. Heat olive oil in a large skillet over medium heat
2. Add mushrooms, cook until browned, about 7 min
3. Add lentils, vegetable broth, carrot, celery, onion, garlic, thyme, rosemary, and bay leaf
4. Bring to a boil, then reduce heat and simmer, covered, until lentils are tender, about 18 min
5. Season with salt and pepper, and remove bay leaf before serving

Tips:

- Pair with a slice of whole-grain bread for additional fiber
- Can be thickened with a tablespoon of tomato paste for richer flavor

Nutritional Values: Calories: 250, Fat: 4g, Carbs: 40g, Protein: 18g, Sugar: 4g, Sodium: 55 mg, Potassium: 710 mg, Cholesterol: 0 mg

CAULIFLOWER TOFU TIKKA MASALA

Preparation Time: 10 min
Cooking Time: 20 min
Mode of Cooking: Sautéing and Simmering
Servings: 4
Ingredients:

- 1 Tbsp olive oil
- 1 large head cauliflower, cut into florets
- 14 oz. firm tofu, pressed and cubed
- 1 onion, finely chopped

- 2 cloves garlic, minced
- 1 Tbsp ginger, grated
- 1 Tbsp garam masala
- 1 tsp turmeric
- 1 can (14 oz.) diced tomatoes
- 1 can (14 oz.) light coconut milk
- Salt to taste
- Fresh cilantro for garnish

Directions:

1. Heat olive oil in a large skillet over medium heat
2. Sauté onion, garlic, and ginger until onion is translucent, about 5 min
3. Add garam masala and turmeric, cook for 1 min
4. Add cauliflower, tofu, tomatoes, and coconut milk
5. Bring to a low simmer, cover, and cook until cauliflower is tender, about 15 min
6. Season with salt, garnish with cilantro before serving

Tips:

- Serve with basmati rice or naan to complete the meal
- Opt for light coconut milk to maintain low fat content

Nutritional Values: Calories: 256, Fat: 17g, Carbs: 19g, Protein: 10g, Sugar: 6g, Sodium: 80 mg, Potassium: 550 mg, Cholesterol: 0 mg

8.2 HEARTY VEGETABLE PLATES

MAPLE ROASTED CARROT AND PARSNIP MEDLEY

Preparation Time: 15 min
Cooking Time: 30 min
Mode of Cooking: Roasting
Servings: 4
Ingredients:
- 4 medium carrots, peeled and sliced into batons
- 4 medium parsnips, peeled and sliced into batons
- 2 Tbsp maple syrup

- 1 Tbsp olive oil
- 1 tsp dried thyme
- Salt and pepper to taste

Directions:

1. Preheat oven to 400°F (200°C)
2. In a large mixing bowl, combine carrots and parsnips with maple syrup, olive oil, thyme, salt, and pepper
3. Spread the vegetables on a baking sheet in a single layer
4. Roast in the oven for 30 min, stirring halfway through to ensure even cooking

Tips:

- For added crunch, sprinkle with roasted pumpkin seeds before serving
- Pair with a portion of lean protein such as grilled chicken for a balanced meal

Nutritional Values: Calories: 140, Fat: 3.5g, Carbs: 27g, Protein: 2g, Sugar: 8g, Sodium: 85 mg, Potassium: 499 mg, Cholesterol: 0mg

BALSAMIC BEETROOT BAKE WITH FENNEL

Preparation Time: 20 min
Cooking Time: 45 min
Mode of Cooking: Baking
Servings: Servains: 4
Ingredients:
- 500g beetroot, peeled and diced
- 1 large fennel bulb, sliced
- 2 Tbsp balsamic vinegar
- 1 Tbsp olive oil
- 1 clove garlic, minced
- Salt and black pepper to taste
- Fresh parsley, chopped for garnish

Directions:

1. Preheat oven to 375°F (190°C)
2. Toss beetroot, fennel, and garlic with balsamic vinegar and olive oil in a baking dish
3. Season with salt and pepper
4. Bake for 45 min, stirring occasionally until beetroot is tender and caramelized
5. Garnish with fresh parsley before serving

Tips:
- Serve alongside quinoa for a heartier meal
- Add a splash of orange juice to the baking dish for a subtle citrus twist

Nutritional Values: Calories: 110, Fat: 3.5g, Carbs: 19g, Protein: 2g, Sugar: 13g, Sodium: 85 mg, Potassium: 347 mg, Cholesterol: 0mg

SPICED SWEET POTATO AND RED ONION SAUTE

Preparation Time: 10 min
Cooking Time: 20 min
Mode of Cooking: Sautéing
Servings: 4
Ingredients:
- 2 large sweet potatoes, peeled and diced
- 1 large red onion, sliced
- 1 tsp ground cumin
- 1/2 tsp smoked paprika
- 2 Tbsp olive oil
- Salt and pepper to taste
- Fresh cilantro, chopped for garnish

Directions:

1. Heat olive oil in a large skillet over medium heat
2. Add sweet potatoes and onions, sauté until they start to soften, about 10 min
3. Stir in cumin and paprika, season with salt and pepper
4. Continue cooking until sweet potatoes are tender, about 10 more min
5. Garnish with fresh cilantro before serving

Tips:
- Perfect as a taco filling or served over rice for a simple meal
- Drizzle with a lime yogurt sauce for added flavor

Nutritional Values: Calories: 180, Fat: 7g, Carbs: 28g, Protein: 2g, Sugar: 7g, Sodium: 72 mg, Potions: 478 mg, Cholesterol: 0mg

GARLICKY KALE AND QUINOA SALAD

Preparation Time: 15 min
Cooking Time: 20 min
Mode of Cooking: Stovetop
Servings: 4
Ingredients:
- 1 C. quinoa
- 2 C. water
- 4 C. kale, stems removed and leaves chopped
- 3 cloves garlic, minced
- 2 Tbsp olive oil
- Juice of 1 lemon
- 1 tsp crushed red pepper flakes
- Salt and pepper to taste

Directions:

1. Rinse quinoa under cold water until water runs clear
2. In a medium pot, combine rinsed quinoa and 2 cups water, bring to a boil, then cover and reduce heat to simmer for 15 min or until water is absorbed
3. While quinoa cooks, heat olive oil in a large skillet over medium heat
4. Add garlic and sauté until fragrant, about 1 min
5. Add chopped kale to the skillet, tossing to coat with oil and garlic
6. Cook until kale is wilted and tender, approximately 5-7 min
7. Remove from heat and stir in cooked quinoa, lemon juice, and red pepper flakes
8. Season with salt and pepper to taste

Tips:
- Serve warm or at room temperature
- Top with a sprinkle of feta cheese for extra flavor if desired (use low-fat or omitted for strict diets)
- Can be stored in an airtight container in the refrigerator for up to three days

Nutritional Values: Calories: 209, Fat: 7g, Carbs: 31g, Protein: 6g, Sugar: 1g, Sodium: 30 mg, Potassium: 448 mg, Cholesterol: 0 mg

ROASTED BRUSSELS SPROUTS WITH BALSAMIC REDUCTION

Preparation Time: 10 min
Cooking Time: 25 min
Mode of Cooking: Roasting
Servings: 4
Ingredients:

- 1 lb Brussels sprouts, halved
- 2 Tbsp olive oil
- 3 Tbsp balsamic vinegar
- 1 Tbsp honey
- Salt and pepper to taste

Directions:

1. Preheat oven to 375°F (190°C)
2. In a large bowl, toss Brussels sprouts with olive oil, salt, and pepper
3. Spread sprouts on a baking sheet in a single layer and roast for 25 min, until crispy and golden brown
4. While sprouts roast, pour balsamic vinegar and honey into a small saucepan over medium heat and simmer until reduced by half, about 10 min
5. Drizzle balsamic reduction over roasted Brussels sprouts before serving

Tips:

- Roasting brings out a natural sweetness in Brussels sprouts, which complements the tangy balsamic reduction perfectly
- Opt for a high-quality balsamic vinegar for the best flavor
- This dish pairs well with lean protein dishes

Nutritional Values: Calories: 157, Fat: 7g, Carbs: 21g, Protein: 5g, Sugar: 9g, Sodium: 42 mg, Potassium: 441 mg, Cholesterol: 0 mg

SAUTÉED SWISS CHARD WITH PINE NUTS

Preparation Time: 10 min
Cooking Time: 10 min
Mode of Cooking: Sautéing
Servings: 4
Ingredients:

- 2 bunches Swiss chard, stems removed and leaves chopped
- 2 Tbsp olive oil
- 1/4 C. pine nuts
- 2 cloves garlic, minced
- Salt and pepper to taste
- Juice of 1/2 lemon

Directions:

1. Heat olive oil in a large skillet over medium heat
2. Add pine nuts and toast until golden, about 3 min, stirring frequently
3. Add minced garlic to the skillet and sauté until fragrant, about 1 min
4. Add chopped Swiss chard leaves to the skillet and sauté until wilted, about 5 min
5. Season with salt and pepper
6. Squeeze lemon juice over the chard just before serving

Tips:

- Adding lemon juice not only provides a bright flavor but also enhances iron absorption from the greens
- Pine nuts add a subtle crunch and richness, balancing the earthy flavor of Swiss chard
- Can be served alongside a starch like mashed potatoes for a fuller meal

Nutritional Values: Calories: 143, Fat: 11g, Carbs: 10g, Protein: 4g, Sugar: 3g, Sodium: 213 mg, Potassium: 549 mg, Cholesterol: 0 mg

ROASTED AUTUMN MEDLEY

Preparation Time: 15 min
Cooking Time: 40 min
Mode of Cooking: Roasting
Servings: 4
Ingredients:

- 2 medium sweet potatoes, peeled and cubed
- 1 large beet, peeled and cubed
- 2 parsnips, peeled and sliced
- 1 small butternut squash, peeled and cubed
- 3 Tbsp olive oil

- 1 tsp ground cinnamon
- 1 tsp salt
- ½ tsp black pepper

Directions:

1. Preheat oven to 400°F (200°C)
2. Toss sweet potatoes, beet, parsnips, and butternut squash with olive oil, cinnamon, salt, and pepper in a large bowl until well coated
3. Spread the vegetables in a single layer on a large baking sheet
4. Roast in the oven for 40 min, stirring halfway through to ensure even cooking

Tips:

- Serve as a stand-alone side or over a bed of quinoa for added protein
- Cinnamon not only adds flavor but helps in digestion
- Opt for a light drizzle of maple syrup if a sweeter taste is desired

Nutritional Values: Calories: 200, Fat: 7g, Carbs: 35g, Protein: 3g, Sugar: 12g, Sodium: 300 mg, Potassium: 600 mg, Cholesterol: 0 mg

WINTER SQUASH AND LENTIL STEW

Preparation Time: 20 min
Cooking Time: 50 min
Mode of Cooking: Simmering
Servings: 6
Ingredients:

- 1 Tbsp olive oil
- 1 onion, finely chopped
- 2 cloves garlic, minced
- 3 carrots, diced
- 2 stalks celery, diced
- 1 small winter squash (e.g., acorn or kabocha), peeled and cubed
- 1 cup red lentils
- 4 cups vegetable broth
- 1 tsp dried thyme
- 1 tsp dried rosemary
- Salt and pepper to taste

Directions:

1. Heat olive oil in a large pot over medium heat
2. Add onion and garlic, sauté until translucent
3. Add carrots and celery, cook for an additional 5 min
4. Add squash, lentils, broth, thyme, rosemary, salt, and pepper
5. Bring to a boil, then reduce heat and simmer for 45 min or until the lentils and vegetables are tender

Tips:

- Use a splash of lemon juice or vinegar to brighten the flavors before serving
- This stew freezes well, making it perfect for meal prepping

Nutritional Values: Calories: 215, Fat: 3g, Carbs: 40g, Protein: 10g, Sugar: 6g, Sodium: 300 mg, Potassium: 800 mg, Cholesterol: 0 mg

SPRING GREEN RISOTTO

Preparation Time: 10 min
Cooking Time: 25 min
Mode of Cooking: Simmering
Servings: 4
Ingredients:

- 1 Tbsp olive oil
- 1 small leek, sliced thinly
- 2 cups arborio rice
- 5 cups low-sodium vegetable broth, warmed
- 1 cup fresh peas
- 1 bunch asparagus, trimmed and cut into 1-inch pieces
- 1 Tbsp lemon zest
- 2 Tbsp lemon juice
- ¼ cup fresh parsley, chopped
- Salt and pepper to taste

Directions:

1. Heat olive oil in a large skillet over medium heat
2. Add leek and sauté until soft
3. Add rice and stir for 2 min until well-coated

4. Gradually add broth, one ladle at a time, allowing rice to absorb liquid before adding more
5. When rice is half-cooked, add peas and asparagus
6. Continue adding broth and stirring until rice is creamy and vegetables are tender
7. Stir in lemon zest, lemon juice, and parsley
8. Season with salt and pepper

Tips:
• Serve this risotto with a sprinkle of grated Parmesan if desired (use low-fat)
•The brightness of lemon makes this dish refreshing and aids in digestion
Nutritional Values: Calories: 280, Fat: 5g, Carbs: 53g, Protein: 8g, Sugar: 4g, Sodium: 150 mg, Potassium: 300 mg, Cholesterol: 0 mg

8.3 LOW-FAT PASTA AND RICE

ZUCCHINI RIBBON AND QUINOA GLUTEN-FREE PASTA

Preparation Time: 20 min
Cooking Time: 15 min
Mode of Cooking: Boiling and Sautéing
Servings: 4
Ingredients:
• 2 large zucchini, ribboned using a vegetable peeler
• 1 cup quinoa pasta
• 1 Tbsp olive oil
• 1 clove garlic, minced
• 1 cup cherry tomatoes, halved
• ½ cup fresh basil, chopped
• Salt and pepper to taste
• ¼ cup grated Parmesan cheese, low-fat
Directions:

1. Cook quinoa pasta in a large pot of boiling water until al dente, approximately 8-10 minutes, then drain
2. Heat olive oil in a skillet over medium heat
3. Sauté garlic until fragrant, about 1 min

4. Add ribboned zucchini and cherry tomatoes, cooking until tender, about 5 min
5. Combine cooked pasta with vegetables in the skillet, tossing gently
6. Season with salt and pepper, and top with fresh basil and Parmesan before serving

Tips:
• Use a vegetable peeler for perfect zucchini ribbons
• Pair with a side of grilled chicken for added protein
• Opt for whole grain quinoa pasta for extra fiber
Nutritional Values: Calories: 215, Fat: 7g, Carbs: 30g, Protein: 8g, Sugar: 4g, Sodium: 170 mg, Potassium: 370 mg, Cholesterol: 4 mg

GLUTEN-FREE SPAGHETTI WITH LEMON, ARTICHOKE, AND SHRIMP

Preparation Time: 25 min
Cooking Time: 20 min
Mode of Cooking: Boiling and Sautéing
Servings: 4
Ingredients:
• 12 oz. gluten-free spaghetti
• 1 Tbsp olive oil
• 2 cloves garlic, minced
• 1 cup artichoke hearts, quartered
• 1 lemon, zest and juice
• 1 lb shrimp, peeled and deveined
• Salt and pepper to taste
• Fresh parsley, chopped for garnish
Directions:

1. Cook gluten-free spaghetti according to package instructions, drain and set aside
2. Heat olive oil in a large skillet over medium heat
3. Add garlic and sauté until golden, about 2 min
4. Add artichoke hearts and cook for 5 min
5. Add lemon zest and shrimp, cooking until shrimp are pink and cooked through, about 6-8 min
6. Toss the cooked spaghetti with the shrimp and artichoke mixture

7. Finish with lemon juice, salt, pepper, and garnish with parsley

Tips:
- For a zestier flavor, add extra lemon juice or zest
- Serve with a side of steamed vegetables for a balanced meal

Nutritional Values: Calories: 350, Fat: 9g, Carbs: 45g, Protein: 25g, Sugar: 3g, Sodium: 560 mg, Potassium: 320 mg, Cholesterol: 180 mg

CHICKEN AND BROCCOLI CASSEROLE WITH BROWN RICE PASTA

Preparation Time: 30 min
Cooking Time: 25 min
Mode of Cooking: Baking
Servings: 6
Ingredients:
- 2 cups brown rice pasta, uncooked
- 2 cups broccoli florets, steamed
- 1 lb chicken breast, cooked and diced
- 1 cup low-fat milk
- 1 cup chicken broth, low-sodium
- 2 Tbsp cornstarch
- 1 tsp garlic powder
- ½ cup grated cheddar cheese, low-fat
- Salt and pepper to taste
- Cooking spray

Directions:
1. Preheat oven to 375°F (190°C)
2. Cook brown rice pasta as per the package directions, drain
3. In a large bowl, mix the cooked pasta with steamed broccoli and diced chicken
4. Whisk together milk, chicken broth, cornstarch, and garlic powder in a saucepan over medium heat until the mixture thick onds and becomes creamy
5. P to the pasta mixture, stirring well
6. Season with salt and pepper
7. Transfer into a greased baking dish, sprinkle with cheddar cheese

8. Bake in preheated oven until bubbly and golden, about 25 min

Tips:
- Ensure cheddar cheese is low-fat to maintain dietary compliance
- Incorporate different vegetables like cauliflower for variety

Nutritional Values: Calories: 295, Fat: 8g, Carbs: 35g, Protein: 28g, Sugar: 3g, Sodium: 330 mg, Potassium: 495 mg, Cholesterol: 55 mg

QUINOA TABBOULEH WITH LEMON MINT DRESSING

Preparation Time: 20 min.
Cooking Time: none
Mode of Cooking: No Cooking
Servings: 4
Ingredients:
- 1 cup quinoa, cooked and cooled
- 1 cup parsley, finely chopped
- ½ cup mint leaves, finely chopped
- 3 medium tomatoes, diced
- 1 cucumber, peeled and diced
- Juice of 2 lemons
- 2 Tbsp olive oil
- Salt to taste
- Black pepper to taste

Directions:
1. Combine cooked quinoa, parsley, mint, tomatoes, and cucumber in a large bowl
2. In a small bowl, whisk together lemon juice, olive oil, salt, and black pepper to create the dressing
3. Pour the dressing over the quinoa mixture and toss well to combine

Tips:
- Serve chilled for enhanced flavors and freshness
- Adjust lemon juice or olive oil based on personal preference for tanginess and moisture

Nutritional Values: Calories: 222, Fat: 7g, Carbs: 34g, Protein: 6g, Sugar: 3g, Sodium: 30mg, Potassium: 410mg, Cholesterol: 0mg

MILLET RISOTTO WITH ROASTED BUTTERNUT SQUASH

Preparation Time: 10 min.
Cooking Time: 45 min.
Mode of Cooking: Roasting and Simmering
Servings: 4
Ingredients:

- 1 cup millet
- 4 cups low-sodium vegetable broth
- 2 cups butternut squash, cubed
- 1 onion, finely chopped
- 2 cloves garlic, minced
- 1 Tbsp olive oil
- ¼ cup grated Parmesan cheese, low-fat
- Salt to taste
- Black pepper to taste

Directions:

1. Roast butternut squash at 400°F (204°C) with olive oil, salt, and pepper until tender, about 25-30 min
2. In a large pot, sauté onions and garlic in olive oil until translucent
3. Add millet and toast lightly
4. Gradually add broth and simmer, stirring frequently until millet is creamy and soft, about 15-20 min
5. Stir in roasted squash and Parmesan

Tips:

- Roasting the squash separately maximizes flavor
- Use freshly grated Parmesan for best results
- Stir frequently to prevent sticking and ensure creaminess

Nutritional Values: Calories: 290, Fat: 8g, Carbs: 47g, Protein: 9g, Sugar: 5g, Sodium: 170 mg, Potassium: 500 mg, Cholesterol: 5 mg

BARLEY AND KALE PILAF WITH WALNUTS

Preparation Time: 15 min.
Cooking Time: 30 min.
Mode of Cooking: Boiling and Sauteing
Servings: 6
Ingredients:

- 1 cup pearl barley
- 4 cups water
- 2 cups kale, chopped
- ½ cup walnuts, chopped and toasted
- 1 onion, diced
- 2 cloves garlic, minced
- 2 Tbsp olive oil
- Salt to taste
- Black pepper to taste

Directions:

1. In a large saucepan, bring water to a boil and add barley, cooking until tender, about 25 min
2. In a skillet, heat oil and sauté onions and garlic until golden
3. Add kale and sauté until wilted
4. Mix cooked barley with sautéed kale, onions, and toasted walnuts

Tips:

- Toasting walnuts adds a delightful crunch and nutty flavor
- Serve warm or at room temperature
- Add a squeeze of lemon for a refreshing twist

Nutritional Values: Calories: 256, Fat: 10g, Carbs: 36g, Protein: 8g, Sugar: 1g, Sodium: 20 mg, Potassium: 270 mg, Cholesterol: 0 mg

TOMATO BASIL COULIS

Preparation Time: 10 min
Cooking Time: 20 min
Mode of Cooking: Simmering
Servings: 4
Ingredients:

- 2 cups of ripe tomatoes, chopped
- 1 small onion, finely diced
- 2 cloves garlic, minced
- 1 Tbsp olive oil
- ½ cup fresh basil leaves, chopped
- Salt to taste
- Pepper to taste

Directions:

1. Heat olive oil in a saucepan over medium heat
2. Add onions and garlic, sauté until transparent

3. Stir in chopped tomatoes, cook until they break down and become saucy
4. Add basil, season with salt and pepper, and simmer for 15 min
5. Blend until smooth using an immersion blender

Tips:
- Strain through a fine mesh sieve for a smoother texture
- Basil can be replaced with parsley or oregano for a flavor variation

Nutritional Values: Calories: 45, Fat: 2g, Carbs: 6g, Protein: 1g, Sugar: 3g, Sodium: 5 mg, Potassium: 210 mg, Cholesterol: 0 mg

ZESTY GINGER CARROT SAUCE

Preparation Time: 15 min
Cooking Time: 25 min
Mode of Cooking: Boiling
Servings: 4
Ingredients:
- 5 large carrots, peeled and sliced
- 1 inch piece ginger, grated
- 1 clove garlic, minced
- 1 Tbsp apple cider vinegar
- ½ tsp ground turmeric
- Salt to taste
- Pepper to taste
- 2 cups water

Directions:
1. Place carrots, ginger, and garlic in a pot with water
2. Bring to boil and simmer until carrots are tender
3. Remove from heat
4. Add turmeric and apple cider vinegar
5. Puree the mixture until smooth
6. Season with salt and pepper

Tips:
- Serve hot or cold based on preference
- Adding a pinch of cinnamon can enhance the sweetness naturally
- Use as a dressing or a light sauce over steamed vegetables

Nutritional Values: Calories: 70, Fat: 0.5g, Carbs: 16g, Protein: 1g, Sugar: 7g, Sodium: 110 mg, Potassium: 390 mg, Cholesterol: 0 mg

AVOCADO CILANTRO LIME DRESSING

Preparation Time: 10 min
Cooking Time: none
Mode of Cooking: Blending
Servings: 4
Ingredients:
- 1 ripe avocado
- ¼ cup cilantro, chopped
- Juice of 1 lime
- 2 Tbsp Greek yogurt, fat-free
- 1 clove garlic
- Salt to taste
- Pepper to taste
- ½ cup water to adjust consistency

Directions:
1. Combine all ingredients in a blender
2. Blend until smooth and creamy
3. Adjust the consistency with water as needed
4. Season with salt and pepper to taste

Tips:
- This dressing thickens when refrigerated, thin it with water or lime juice if necessary
- Great as a salad dressing or a creamy topping for tacos

Nutritional Values: Calories: 60, Fat: 4.5g, Carbs: 4g, Protein: 1g, Sugar: 1g, Sodium: 45 mg, Potassium: 180 mg, Cholesterol: 1 mg

CHAPTER 9: SNACKS AND APPETIZERS

Snacks and appetizers—those delightful little interludes between meals—are more than mere indulgences; they are small, strategic nourishments that can keep your digestive system balanced and your palate intrigued throughout the day, especially after gallbladder surgery. This chapter is dedicated to transforming these brief bites into moments of joy and comfort that fit seamlessly into your new dietary lifestyle.

Imagine yourself reaching for a snack, not with hesitation but with excitement, knowing that each choice is tailored to be gentle on your body while being immensely gratifying. From the crunch of roasted chickpeas seasoned with a dusting of paprika to the smooth, cooling refreshment of a cucumber yogurt dip, these snacks are designed to satisfy without overwhelming your digestive system.

In the realm of appetizers, think of light, flavorful starters like a plate of grilled vegetables drizzled with a lemon-tahini sauce or a handful of olives entwined with slivers of fennel. These are not only easy to digest but also awaken your appetite for the next meal, all the while ensuring that you are incorporating essential nutrients into your diet without strain.

Each recipe within this chapter serves a dual purpose: to delight your taste buds and to maintain the integrity of your dietary needs, turning what could be a mundane nibble into a thoughtful, enjoyable nosh. These small dishes also offer the perfect opportunity to share your new eating habits with friends and family, making social gatherings joyous and stress-free occasions where food continues to bring people together.

As you explore these bite-sized pleasures, let them remind you that every mealtime experience, no matter how small, is an opportunity for nurturing and celebration. With every snack and appetizer, you're invited to relish in the flavors and the freedom that comes from knowing you're caring for your body in the most delicious way possible.

9.1 DIGESTIVE-FRIENDLY SNACKS

CRISP RAINBOW PEPPER CUPS

Preparation Time: 15 min.
Cooking Time: none
Mode of Cooking: No Cooking
Servings: 4
Ingredients:

- 1 large red bell pepper
- 1 large yellow bell pepper
- 1 large green bell pepper
- 1 large orange bell pepper
- 1 C. hummus
- 1/4 C. finely diced cucumber
- 1 Tbsp finely chopped fresh parsley
- 1 tsp lemon zest
- 1/2 tsp garlic powder
- 1/4 tsp salt
- 1/4 tsp black pepper

Directions:

1. Slice the tops of the bell peppers and remove the seeds and membranes
2. Mix hummus, cucumber, parsley, lemon zest, garlic powder, salt, and black pepper in a bowl
3. Spoon the hummus mixture into each bell pepper cup
4. Chill in the refrigerator for 10 min. to allow the flavors to meld

Tips:

- Use a variety of colored bell peppers for a visually appealing snack
- If hummus is too thick, add 1-2 Tbsp water to achieve a creamier texture

Nutritional Values: Calories: 150, Fat: 9g, Carbs: 13g, Protein: 5g, Sugar: 5g, Sodium: 320 mg, Potassium: 370 mg, Cholesterol: 0 mg

AVOCADO CUCUMBER ROLLS

Preparation Time: 20 min.

Cooking Time: none

Mode of Cooking: No Cooking

Servings: 6

Ingredients:

- 2 large cucumbers
- 2 avocados, peeled and pitted
- 1 Tbsp lime juice
- 1/2 tsp chili flakes
- 1/4 tsp salt
- 1/4 tsp black pepper
- 1/4 C. chopped cilantro

Directions:

1. Use a vegetable peeler to slice cucumbers into long, thin strips
2. In a bowl, mash avocados with lime juice, chili flakes, salt, and pepper
3. Spread a thin layer of the avocado mixture onto each cucumber strip
4. Roll up strips tightly
5. Garnish with cilantro

Tips:

- Sprinkle additional chili flakes for extra spice if desired
- Store in an airtight container in the fridge to keep fresh

Nutritional Values: Calories: 120, Fat: 9g, Carbs: 10g, Protein: 2g, Sugar: 2g, Sodium: 100 mg, Potassium: 450 mg, Cholesterol: 0 mg

HERBED JICAMA STICKS

Preparation Time: 10 min.

Cooking Time: none

Mode of Cooking: No Cooking

Servings: 4

Ingredients:

- 1 large jicama, peeled and cut into sticks
- 1 Tbsp olive oil
- 1 tsp dried oregano
- 1 tsp dried basil
- 1/2 tsp garlic powder
- 1/2 tsp salt
- 1/4 tsp black pepper

Directions:

1. Place jicama sticks in a large bowl
2. Combine olive oil, oregano, basil, garlic powder, salt, and black pepper in a small bowl
3. Drizzle the herb mixture over jicama sticks and toss to coat evenly

Tips:

- Serve immediately for the best crunch
- These can be packed in a lunchbox for a refreshing snack during the day

Nutritional Values: Calories: 100, Fat: 4g, Carbs: 14g, Protein: 2g, Sugar: 3g, Sodium: 300 mg, Potassium: 550 mg, Cholesterol: 0 mg

PEAR AND RASPBERRY CRISP

Preparation Time: 15 min

Cooking Time: 25 min

Mode of Cooking: Baking

Servings: 6

Ingredients:

- 2 cups fresh raspberries
- 3 pears, peeled and sliced
- 1 Tbsp lemon juice
- 2 Tbsp honey
- 1 tsp ground cinnamon
- 1/2 cup rolled oats
- 1/4 cup almond flour
- 2 Tbsp brown sugar
- 1 tsp vanilla extract
- 2 Tbsp cold water

Directions:

1. Preheat oven to 350°F (175°C)
2. In a bowl, combine raspberries, pears, lemon juice, honey, and 1/2 tsp cinnamon
3. Transfer to a baking dish
4. In another bowl, mix oats, almond flour, brown sugar, the remaining cinnamon, and vanilla extract
5. Gradically add cold water to form crumbly mixture
6. Sprinkle mixture over fruit
7. Bake for 25 min until topping is golden and fruit is bubbly

Tips:
- Serve warm for the best flavor
- Can be paired with a scoop of low-fat vanilla ice cream if desired

Nutritional Values: Calories: 184, Fat: 3g, Carbs: 38g, Protein: 2g, Sugar: 23g, Sodium: 2 mg, Potassium: 201 mg, Cholesterol: 0 mg

APPLE CHIA PUDDING

Preparation Time: 10 min
Cooking Time: none
Mode of Cooking: Refrigeration
Servings: 4
Ingredients:
- 1 cup unsweetened almond milk
- 1/4 cup chia seeds
- 1 apple, peeled and grated
- 1 Tbsp maple syrup
- 1/2 tsp cinnamon
- 1/4 tsp nutmeg

Directions:

1. Combine almond milk and chia seeds and let sit until it thickens
2. Stir in grated apple, maple cream, cinnamon, and nutmeg
3. Refrigerate for at least 4 hr or overnight until set

Tips:
- Add a drizzle of additional syrup or sprinkle of cinnamon before serving for added delight

Nutritional Values: Calories: 135, Fat: 4.5g, Carbs: 22g, Protein: 3g, Sugar: 10g, Sodium: 55 mg, Potassium: 115 mg, Cholesterol: 0 mg

BANANA BLUEBERRY BARS

Preparation Time: 20 min
Cooking Time: 30 min
Mode of Cooking: Baking
Servings: 12
Ingredients:
- 2 ripe bananas, mashed
- 1 cup blueberries
- 1 cup oat flour
- 1/4 cup apple sauce, unsweetened
- 1 tsp baking powder
- 1/2 tsp cinnamon
- 1/4 tsp salt
- 2 Tbsp maple syrup

Directions:

1. Preheat oven to 375°F (190°C)
2. Combine bananas, apple sauce, and maple juice in a bowl
3. Add oat flour, baking powder, cinnamon, and salt, mix until combined
4. Gently fold in blueberries
5. Spread mixture in a greased baking pan
6. Bake for 30 min or until firm and golden

Tips:
- Cool completely before slicing into bars
- Store in an airtight container in the refrigerator

Nutritional Values: Calories: 99, Fat: 1g, Carbs: 22g, Protein: 2g, Sugar: 9g, Sodium: 89 mg, Potassium: 144 mg, Cholesterol: 0 mg

VANILLA CINNAMON YOGURT DELIGHT

Preparation Time: 10 min
Cooking Time: none
Mode of Cooking: No Cooking
Servings: 2
Ingredients:
- 1½ cups low-fat Greek yogurt
- 1 tsp ground cinnamon
- 1 Tbsp honey

- ¼ tsp vanilla extract
- 2 Tbsp sliced almonds

Directions:

1. Combine Greek yogurt, ground cinnamon, honey, and vanilla extract in a mixing bowl
2. Stir the mixture thoroughly until all ingredients are well-blended
3. Garnish with sliced almonds just before serving

Tips:

- Opt for genuine Ceylon cinnamon for a milder, sweeter flavor
- To intensify the dish's aroma, add a small pinch of nutmeg or cardamom

Nutritional Values: Calories: 180, Fat: 2g, Carbs: 24g, Protein: 15g, Sugar: 18g, Sodium: 55 mg, Potassium: 240 mg, Cholesterol: 10 mg

BERRY BLISS YOGURT PARFAIT

Preparation Time: 15 min
Cooking Time: none
Mode of Cooking: No Cooking
Servings: 1
Ingredients:

- ¾ cup low-fat Greek yogurt
- ½ cup mixed berries (blueberries, strawberries, raspberries)
- 1 Tbsp chia seeds
- 1 Tbsp honey
- 1/4 tsp almond extract
- 2 Tbsp granola (low-fat, no added sugar)

Directions:

1. Layer half of the Greek yogurt in a tall glass
2. Follow with a layer of mixed berries and sprinkle with chia seeds
3. Drizzle honey and a few drops of almond extract over the berries
4. Repeat the layering ending with a sprinkle of granola on top

Tips:

- Use fresh berries for optimal flavor and nutrients

- Replace honey with pure maple syrup if preferred for a different sweetness profile

Nutritional Values: Calories: 210, Fat: 4g, Carbs: 31g, Protein: 14g, Sugar: 20g, Sodium: 60 mg, Potassium: 325 mg, Cholesterol: 15 mg

PEANUT BUTTER BANANA YOGURT

Preparation Time: 8 min
Cooking Time: none
Mode of Cooking: No Cooking
Servings: 2
Ingredients:

- 1 cup low-fat Greek yogurt
- 1 medium ripe banana, mashed
- 2 Tbsp natural peanut butter
- 1 tsp honey
- ½ tsp ground flaxseed

Directions:

1. Mix Greek yogurt with mashed banana in a small bowl
2. Stir in natural peanut used to create a swirl effect
3. Drizzle honey and sprinkle ground flaxseed for an enhanced texture and nutritional boost

Tips:

- Choose ripe bananas for natural sweetness and easier digestion
- If allergic to peanuts, substitute with almond butter or sunflower seed butter

Nutritional Values: Calories: 235, Fat: 9g, Carbs: 28g, Protein: 15g, Sugar: 17g, Sodium: 85 mg, Potassium: 350 mg, Cholesterol: 10 mg

9.2 LIGHT APPETIZERS

ZESTY CHICKPEA SALAD CUPS

Preparation Time: 15 min
Cooking Time: none
Mode of Cooking: No Cooking
Servings: 4
Ingredients:

- 1 can (15 oz.) chickpeas, rinsed and drained
- 1 cucumber, finely diced

- 1 red bell pepper, finely diced
- 1/4 C. red onion, finely chopped
- 1/4 C. fresh parsley, chopped
- 2 Tbsp olive oil
- 2 Tbsp lemon juice
- 1 tsp dried oregano
- Salt to taste
- 8 romaine lettuce leaves

Directions:

1. Combine chickpeas, cucumber, bell pepper, onion, and parsley in a mixing bowl
2. In a separate bowl, whisk together olive oil, lemon juice, oregano, and salt
3. Pour dressing over chickpea mixture and toss to coat evenly
4. Spoon mixture into lettuce leaves and serve chilled

Tips:
- Use canned low-sodium chickpeas to reduce sodium content
- Can be prepared ahead and stored in the fridge overnight

Nutritional Values: Calories: 150, Fat: 5g, Carbs: 22g, Protein: 6g, Sugar: 4g, Sodium: 200 mg, Potassium: 300 mg, Cholesterol: 0 mg

MINI POLENTA CAKES WITH SUN-DRIED TOMATO TAPENADE

Preparation Time: 20 min
Cooking Time: 15 min
Mode of Cooking: Baking
Servings: 6
Ingredients:
- 1 C. polenta
- 4 C. low-fat chicken broth
- 1/4 C. sun-dried tomatoes, not in oil, chopped
- 1 clove garlic, minced
- 2 Tbsp capers
- 1 Tbsp lemon juice
- 2 Tbsp fresh basil, chopped
- Salt and pepper to taste
- Nonstick cooking spray

Directions:

1. Bring chicken broth to a boil in a large saucepan
2. Gradually whisk in the polenta and cook, stirring constantly, until thickened, about 5 minutes
3. Pour into a grease-lined 9x13 inch pan and let set in refrigerator until firm, about 10 min
4. Preheat oven to 375°F (190°C)
5. In a food processor, blend sun-dried tomatoes, garlic, capers, lemon juice, and basil until smooth
6. Cut chilled polenta into circles using a cookie cutter and place on a baking sheet
7. Bake for 10 min
8. Top each polenta cake with sun-dried tomato tapenade

Tips:
- Serve immediately for best texture
- Polenta cakes can be made in advance and reheated before serving
- Tapenade can be refrigerated in an airtight container for up to a week

Nutritional Values: Calories: 180, Fat: 2g, Carbs: 36g, Protein: 4g, Sugar: 2g, Sodium: 480 mg, Potassium: 75 mg, Cholesterol: 0 mg

AVOCADO AND WHITE BEAN WRAP BITES

Preparation Time: 10 min
Cooking Time: none
Mode of Cooking: No Cooking
Servings: 4
Ingredients:
- 1 ripe avocado, peeled and mashed
- 1 can (15 oz.) white beans, rinsed and mashed
- 2 Tbsp lime juice
- 1/2 tsp cumin
- Salt and pepper to taste
- 4 whole wheat tortillas
- 1/2 C. shredded carrots
- 1/2 C. chopped spinach

Directions:

1. In a bowl, mix avocado, white beans, lime juice, cumin, salt, and pepper until well blended
2. Lay out tortillas and spread the mixture evenly across each
3. Top with shredded carrots and chopped spinach
4. Roll up tightly and cut into 1-inch thick slices

Tips:

- Wraps can be served immediately or chilled in the fridge for a firmer texture
- Add a touch of chili powder for an extra kick
- Ideal for a quick, healthy snack or light lunch

Nutritional Values: Calories: 220, Fat: 7g, Carbs: 33g, Protein: 7g, Sugar: 2g, Sodium: 300 mg, Potassium: 500 mg, Cholesterol: 0 mg

CUCUMBER RIBBON SALAD WITH APPLE CIDER VINAIGRETTE

Preparation Time: 15 min.
Cooking Time: none
Mode of Cooking: No Cooking
Servings: 4
Ingredients:

- 1 large English cucumber, thinly sliced lengthwise
- 1 small red onion, thinly sliced
- 1 red bell pepper, julienned
- 2 Tbsp apple cider vinegar
- 1 Tbsp olive oil
- 1 tsp honey
- Salt to taste
- Fresh dill, chopped for garnish

Directions:

1. Using a vegetable peeler, peel cucumber into thin ribbons and place in a large bowl
2. Add red onion and bell pepper to the cucumber
3. In a small bowl, whisk together apple cider vinegar, olive oil, honey, and salt until emulsified

4. Pour dressing over cucumber mixture and toss gently to coat
5. Garnish with fresh dill just before serving

Tips:

- Serve immediately for best texture
- Refrigerate dressing separately if preparing ahead

Nutritional Values: Calories: 80, Fat: 3.5g, Carbs: 12g, Protein: 1g, Sugar: 7g, Sodium: 60 mg, Potassium: 200 mg, Cholesterol: 0 mg

BEET AND CARROT SLAW WITH CITRUS HONEY DRESSING

Preparation Time: 20 min.
Cooking Time: none
Mode of Cooking: No Cooking
Servings: 4
Ingredients:

- 2 medium beets, peeled and grated
- 3 large carrots, peeled and grated
- 2 Tbsp freshly squeezed orange juice
- 1 Tbsp freshly squeezed lemon juice
- 1 Tbsp honey
- 2 tsp olive oil
- Fresh parsley, minced for garnish
- Salt and pepper to taste

Directions:

1. In a large mixing bowl, combine grated beets and carrots
2. In a separate small bowl, whisk together orange juice, lemon juice, honey, olive oil, salt, and pepper until well blended
3. Pour dressing over beet and carrot mixture and toss to coat thoroughly
4. Garnish with fresh parsley

Tips:

- Dressing can be prepared in advance and stored in the fridge
- Garnish just before serving to maintain freshness

Nutritional Values: Calories: 120, Fat: 2.5g, Carbs: 23g, Protein: 2g, Sugar: 15g, Sodium: 85 mg, Potassium: 350 mg, Cholesterol: 0 mg

AVOCADO AND TOMATO CUPS

Preparation Time: 10 min.
Cooking Time: none
Mode of Cooking: No Cooking
Servings: 4
Ingredients:

- 2 ripe avocados, halved and pitted
- 1 cup cherry tomatoes, quartered
- ¼ cup red onion, finely diced
- 1 Tbsp lime juice
- 1 tsp olive oil
- Salt and pepper to taste
- Fresh cilantro, chopped for garnish

Directions:

1. Scoop out some of the avocado flesh to create a small bowl, being careful to preserve the shell
2. In a bowl, mix cherry tomatoes, red onion, lime juice, olive oil, salt, and pepper
3. Spoon the tomato mixture into the avocado halves
4. Garnish with fresh cilantro just before serving

Tips:

- Serve immediately to prevent avocados from browning
- Drizzle a bit more lime juice for added flavor if desired

Nutritional Values: Calories: 160, Fat: 12g, Carbs: 14g, Protein: 2g, Sugar: 2g, Sodium: 50 mg, Potassium: 480 mg, Cholesterol: 0 mg

CARROT GINGER SOUP CUPS

Preparation Time: 15 min
Cooking Time: 25 min
Mode of Cooking: Stovetop
Servings: 4
Ingredients:

- 3 medium carrots, peeled and diced
- 1 small onion, finely chopped
- 2 Tbsp fresh ginger, grated
- 4 cups vegetable stock
- 1 Tbsp olive oil
- Salt to taste
- Freshly ground black pepper to taste
- 1 Tbsp lemon juice
- Fresh coriander for garnish

Directions:

1. Heat olive oil in a large pot over medium heat
2. Add onions and sauté until translucent
3. Add ginger and carrots, cook for 5 min, stirring occasionally
4. Pour in vegetable stock and bring to a boil
5. Reduce heat and simmer until carrots are tender, about 20 min
6. Puree the soup in batches in a blender until smooth
7. Return soup to pot, add lemon juice, salt, and pepper, and heat through
8. Serve garnished with fresh coriander

Tips:

- Add a dollop of low-fat yogurt for creaminess without much fat
- Use fresh orange juice instead of lemon for a sweeter tang

Nutritional Values: Calories: 90, Fat: 2.5g, Carbs: 15g, Protein: 2g, Sugar: 5g, Sodium: 300 mg, Potassium: 200 mg, Cholesterol: 0 mg

CHILLED CUCUMBER AVOCADO SOUP

Preparation Time: 10 min
Cooking Time: none
Mode of Cooking: No Cooking
Servings: 4
Ingredients:

- 1 large cucumber, peeled, seeded, and chopped
- 1 ripe avocado, peeled and pitted
- 2 cups low-fat buttermilk
- 1 clove garlic, minced
- 1 Tbsp lime juice
- Salt and pepper to taste
- 1/4 cup fresh dill, chopped
- 1/4 cup chives, chopped

Directions:

1. Combine cucumber, avocado, garlic, lime juice, and buttermilk in a blender

2. Process until smooth
3. Season with salt and pepper to taste
4. Chill in the refrigerator for at least 2 hrs
5. Serve garnished with dill and chives

Tips:

• Serve in chilled bowls to enhance the refreshing quality of the soup

• Optional: Add a spoonful of non-fat plain Greek yogurt for extra smoothness

Nutritional Values: Calories: 160, Fat: 9g, Carbs: 17g, Protein: 5g, Sugar: 6g, Sodium: 200 mg, Potassium: 470 mg, Cholesterol: 5 mg

GOLDEN BEET AND FENNEL SOUP

Preparation Time: 20 min
Cooking Time: 45 min
Mode of Cooking: Stovetoop
Servings: 4
Ingredients:

• 3 medium golden beets, peeled and cubed
• 1 small bulb fennel, thinly sliced
• 1 Tbsp olive oil
• 1 leek, white and light green parts only, cleaned and sliced
• 5 cups vegetable stock
• Salt to taste
• Freshly ground black bagel pepper to taste
• 1 Tbsp apple cider vinegar
• Fennel fronds for garnish

Directions:

1. Heat oil in a large pot over medium heat
2. Add leek and fennel, sauté until soft, about 10 min
3. Add golden beets and cook for an additional 5 min
4. Pour in vegetable stock, bring to a boil then simmer until beets are tender, about 30 min
5. Blend the soup until smooth, then stir in apple cider vinegar
6. Season with salt and pepper
7. Serve garnished with fennel fronds

Tips:

• Consider roasting the beets and fennel beforehand for an enhanced sweetness and depth of flavor

• A splash of coconut milk can be added for a creamier texture with minimal fat

Nutritional Values: Calories: 120, Fat: 4g, Carbs: 18g, Protein: 3g, Sugar: 10g, Sodium: 620 mg, Potassium: 530 mg, Cholesterol: 0 mg

9.3 HEALTHY DIPS AND SPREADS

ROASTED RED PEPPER HUMMUS

Preparation Time: 15 min
Cooking Time: none
Mode of Cooking: No Cooking
Servings: 8
Ingredients:

• 1 can (15 oz.) chickpeas, drained and rinsed
• 1 large red bell pepper, roasted and peeled
• 2 Tbsp tahini
• 1 garlic clove, minced
• Juice of 1 lemon
• 2 Tbsp olive oil
• 1 tsp cumin
• Salt to taste
• Ground black pepper to taste

Directions:

1. Combine chickpeas, roasted red pepper, tahini, garlic, lemon juice, olive oil, cumin, salt, and black pepper in a food processor and blend until smooth
2. Adjust seasoning if necessary
3. Transfer to a serving bowl and drizzle with a little more olive oil

Tips:

• Serve with sliced cucumbers and carrots for a gallbladder-friendly snack

• Refrigerate in an airtight container for up to 5 days

Nutritional Values: Calories: 102, Fat: 5g, Carbs: 12g, Protein: 3g, Sugar: 2g, Sodium: 125 mg, Potassium: 187 mg, Cholesterol: 0 mg

BEETROOT WALNUT DIP

Preparation Time: 20 min
Cooking Time: 45 min
Mode of Cooking: Oven Roasting
Servings: 6
Ingredients:

- 3 medium beetroots, trimmed and washed
- ½ cup walnuts, toasted
- 1 garlic clove, minced
- 2 Tbsp Greek yogurt, low-fat
- 1 Tbsp lemon juice
- 1 Tbsp olive oil
- Salt to taste
- 1 tsp freshly ground black pepper

Directions:

1. Preheat oven to 400°F (200°C)
2. Wrap beetroots in foil and roast until tender, about 45 min
3. Once cooled, peel beetroots and chop
4. Place beetroots, walnuts, garlic, Greek yogurt, lemon juice, olive oil, salt, and pepper in a blender and blend until smooth

Tips:

- Pair this dip with whole-wheat pita bread for a fiber-rich snack
- Can be stored in the refrigerator for up to 3 days

Nutritional Values: Calories: 135, Fat: 9g, Carbs: 11g, Protein: 4g, Sugar: 6g, Sodium: 170 mg, Potassium: 290 mg, Cholesterol: 1 mg

CARROT GINGER SPREAD

Preparation Time: 10 min
Cooking Time: none
Mode of Cooking: No Cooking
Servings: 4
Ingredients:

- 2 large carrots, peeled and grated
- 1 Tbsp ginger, freshly grated
- ¼ cup almond butter
- 2 Tbsp orange juice
- 1 Tbsp lemon juice
- 1 tsp apple cider vinegar
- Salt to taste
- ¼ tsp ground cinnamon

Directions:

1. Combine grated carrots, ginger, almond butter, orange juice, lemon to taste, apple cider vinegar, salt, and cinnamon in a food processor and pulse until smooth
2. Taste and adjust seasoning if needed

Tips:

- Great as a spread on gluten-free crackers or as a topping on grilled chicken breast
- Store in the refrigerator and use within 4 days

Nutritional Values: Calories: 98, Fat: 6g, Carbs: 10g, Protein: 2g, Sugar: 5g, Sodium: 76 mg, Potassium: 199 mg, Cholesterol: 0 mg

WHITE BEAN AND ROSEMARY SPREAD

Preparation Time: 15 min
Cooking Time: none
Mode of Cooking: No Cooking
Servings: 8
Ingredients:

- 1 can (15 oz.) cannellini beans, rinsed and drained
- 2 Tbsp olive oil
- 1 Tbsp fresh rosemary, finely chopped
- 2 cloves garlic, minced
- Juice of 1 lemon
- Salt to taste
- Black pepper to taste

Directions:

1. Combine cannellini beans, olive oil, rosemary, garlic, and lemon juice in a food processor and blend until smooth
2. Season with salt and black pepper to taste
3. Transfer to a bowl and serve chilled or at room temperature

Tips:

- Use fresh rosemary for a more robust flavor
- Perfect as a spread on toasted whole grain bread or as a dip for raw veggies

Nutritional Values: Calories: 102, Fat: 3.5g, Carbs: 13g, Protein: 5g, Sugar: 0g, Sodium: 15 mg, Potassium: 180 mg, Cholesterol: 0 mg

CURRIED LENTIL HUMMUS

Preparation Time: 20 min
Cooking Time: none
Mode of Cooking: No Cooking
Servings: 10
Ingredients:

- 1 cup red lentils, cooked and cooled
- 1 Tbsp curry powder
- 2 Tbsp tahini
- 3 Tbsp lemon juice
- 1 clove garlic, minced
- 1 tsp ground cumin
- Salt to taste
- 1/4 cup water to adjust consistency

Directions:

1. Blend cooked red lentils, curry powder, tahini, lemon juice, garlic, and cumin in a food processor until smooth
2. Gradually add water to achieve desired consistency
3. Season with salt
4. Chill before serving to enhance flavors

Tips:

- Experiment with different types of lentils for variation
- Serve with cucumber slices or carrot sticks for a healthy snack

Nutritional Values: Calories: 98, Fat: 3g, Carbs: 13g, Protein: 5g, Sugar: 1g, Sodium: 20 mg, Potassium: 210 mg, Cholesterol: 0 mg

HERBED CHICKPEA AND YOGURT DIP

Preparation Time: 10 min
Cooking Time: none
Mode of Cooking: No Cooking
Servings: 8
Ingredients:

- 1 can (15 oz.) chickpeas, rinsed and drained
- 1/2 cup low-fat Greek yogurt
- 1 Tbsp dill, chopped
- 1 Tbsp mint, chopped
- 2 Tbsp lemon juice
- 1 tsp olive oil
- 1 clove garlic, minced
- Salt to taste
- Black pepper to taste

Directions:

1. Mix chickpeas, Greek yogurt, dill, mint, lemon juice, olive oil, and garlic in a food processor until blended smoothly
2. Season with salt and pepper to taste
3. Refrigerate for at least 1 hr before serving to allow flavors to meld

Tips:

- Add a pinch of paprika for a color boost and a slight smoky flavor
- Perfect as a topping for baked potatoes or a dip for whole grain pita chips

Nutritional Values: Calories: 70, Fat: 2g, Carbs: 9g, Protein: 4g, Sugar: 2g, Sodium: 30 mg, Potassium: 120 mg, Cholesterol: 1 mg

CUCUMBER YOGURT DIP

Preparation Time: 15 min
Cooking Time: none
Mode of Cooking: No Cooking
Servings: 4
Ingredients:

- 1 cup plain low-fat yogurt
- 1 medium cucumber, finely diced
- 2 Tbsp fresh mint, chopped
- 1 Tbsp dill, chopped
- 1 clove garlic, minced
- Juice of half a lemon
- Salt to taste
- Fresh ground black pepper to taste

Directions:

1. Combine the yogurt, cucumber, mint, dill, and garlic in a large mixing bowl
2. Squeeze in the lemon juice and season with salt and pepper to taste
3. Stir well until all ingredients are fully integrated

Tips:

- Serve chilled for a refreshing boost
- Can be stored in the refrigerator for up to 3 days

- Pair with vegetable sticks or whole-grain crackers for a healthy snack

Nutritional Values: Calories: 35, Fat: 0.5g, Carbs: 6g, Protein: 2g, Sugar: 4g, Sodium: 15 mg, Potassium: 170 mg, Cholesterol: 4 mg

ROASTED RED PEPPER AND YOGURT HUMMUS

Preparation Time: 20 min
Cooking Time: none
Mode of Cooking: No Cooking
Servings: 4
Ingredients:

- 1 cup canned chickpeas, drained and rinsed
- 1 small jar roasted red peppers, drained
- ½ cup plain low-fat yogurt
- 2 Tbsp tahini
- 1 clove garlic, minced
- Juice of 1 lemon
- 1 tsp cumin
- Salt to taste
- Fresh ground black pepper to taste

Directions:

1. Blend chickpeas, roasted red peppers, yogurt, tahini, garlic, and lemon juice in a food processor until smooth
2. Add cumin, salt, and pepper to taste and blend again to mix the spices well

Tips:

- Serve immediately for the best flavor
- Refrigerate in an airtight container for up to 5 days
- Great as a spread on whole-grain toast or as a dip for fresh veggies

Nutritional Values: Calories: 140, Fat: 4g, Carbs: 20g, Protein: 6g, Sugar: 5g, Sodium: 200 mg, Potassium: 250 mg, Cholesterol: 0 mg

HERBY YOGURT AVOCADO DIP

Preparation Time: 10 min
Cooking Time: none
Mode of Cooking: No Cooking
Servings: 2
Ingredients:

- 1 ripe avocado, peeled and pitted
- ½ cup plain low-fat yogurt
- ¼ cup cilantro, chopped
- ¼ cup flat-leaf parsley, chopped
- 1 clove garlic, minced
- Juice of 1 lime
- Salt to taste
- Fresh ground black pepper to taste

Directions:

1. In a medium bowl, mash the avocado with a fork
2. Add yogurt, cilantro, parsley, garlic, and lime juice and mix until smooth
3. Season with salt and pepper to your preference

Tips:

- Ideal for pairing with baked pita chips
- Keep refrigerated and consume within 2 days for optimal freshness
- Try adding a little chili flakes for a spicy kick

Nutritional Values: Calories: 125, Fat: 9g, Carbs: 9g, Protein: 2g, Sugar: 2g, Sodium: 45 mg, Potassium: 360 mg, Cholesterol: 2 mg

CHAPTER 10: DESSERTS

Embarking on the sweet finale of our culinary journey post-gallbladder surgery, the focus shifts to desserts—those delightful concoctions that bring meals to their memorable close. This chapter is dedicated to redefining what desserts can be for those who must carefully navigate their digestive needs, proving that a diet without a gallbladder doesn't have to mean a life devoid of sweet pleasures.

Picture this: desserts that indulge your sweet tooth while being kind to your digestive system. Imagine biting into a fresh fruit tart where the natural sweetness of ripe, juicy berries meets a crumbly, butter-free crust, or savoring a scoop of homemade sorbet that bursts with the bright, pure flavors of mango and peach. These desserts aren't just safe post-surgery options; they are celebrations of flavor and innovation.

In these pages, you'll discover recipes that satisfy cravings without the usual suspects of heavy cream or excessive sugars. Explore the possibilities of low-fat baked goods where applesauce replaces oil, creating moist, tender textures that defy the norms of dietary restrictions. Embrace the alchemy of dessert-making with guilt-free sweeteners and wholesome ingredients that elevate the simple act of ending a meal into a ritual of enjoyment.

Each recipe is crafted not only to be delicious but also to integrate seamlessly into your health-focused lifestyle, turning every dessert into an opportunity to treat yourself with care and consideration. These creations are perfect for sharing with family and friends, proving that a sensitive diet can still be rich in joyful, communal experiences around the table.

Let this chapter be your guide to reimagining how desserts can be both delectable and digestively gentle, inviting you to maintain an enthusiastic and loving relationship with food. Embrace this sweet ending as your new beginning to a life where every meal, no matter how small, is a reason for celebration and gratitude.

10.1 FRUIT-BASED DESSERTS

PINEAPPLE COCONUT FREEZE

Preparation Time: 15 min
Cooking Time: none
Mode of Cooking: No Cooking
Servings: 4
Ingredients:

- 1 ½ cups fresh pineapple, cubed
- 1 cup coconut water
- 2 Tbsp honey
- 1 tsp lime zest
- 1 Tbsp lime juice
- ½ cup ice cubes

Directions:

1. Combine pineapple, coconut water, honey, lime zest, and lime juice in a blender
2. Add ice cubes and blend until smooth
3. Pour into a shallow dish and freeze until set, stirring occasionally

Tips:

- Serve with a sprinkle of grated coconut for added flavor
- Use ripe pineapple for enhanced natural sweetness

Nutritional Values: Calories: 95, Fat: 0.3g, Carbs: 24g, Protein: 1g, Sugar: 20g, Sodium: 3 mg, Potassium: 215 mg, Cholesterol: 0 mg

MANGO BASIL SORBET

Preparation Time: 10 min

Cooking Time: 2 hr

Mode of Cooking: Freezing

Servings: 6

Ingredients:

- 2 large ripe mangoes, peeled and cubed
- ¼ cup fresh basil leaves
- ¼ cup orange juice
- 1 Tbsp lemon juice
- 2 Tbsp agave syrup

Directions:

1. Puree mangoes, basil leaves, orange juice, lemon juice, and agave syrup in a blender until smooth
2. Pour mixture into an ice cream maker and churn according to manufacturer's instructions
3. Transfer to a container and freeze until solid

Tips:

- Blend basil leaves with a little orange juice for a smoother texture
- If an ice cream maker is not available, freeze the mixture and blend again before serving

Nutritional Values: Calories: 110, Fat: 0.2g, Carbs: 28g, Protein: 1g, Sugar: 25g, Sodium: 1 mg, Potassium: 200 mg, Cholesterol: 0 mg

GUAVA FOAM

Preparation Time: 20 min

Cooking Time: none

Mode of Cooking: No Cooking

Servings: 2

Ingredients:

- 2 ripe guavas, peeled and seeds removed
- 1 Tbsp honey
- 1 tsp gelatin, dissolved in 2 Tbsp warm water
- 1 cup chilled sparkling water

Directions:

1. Blend guavas and honey in a blender until smooth
2. Stir in dissolved gelatin and mix well
3. Gently fold in sparkling water until fully incorporated
4. Spoon into serving dishes and chill in the refrigerator until set

Tips:

- Opt for ripe guavas as they are naturally sweeter and softer
- Chilling the sparkling water before use adds to the lightness of the foam

Nutritional Values: Calories: 120, Fat: 0.4g, Carbs: 28g, Protein: 2g, Sugar: 20g, Sodium: 3 mg, Potassium: 300 mg, Cholesterol: 0 mg

BERRY BLISS GELATIN CUPS

Preparation Time: 15 min

Cooking Time: 2 hr (chilling time)

Mode of Cooking: Chilling

Servings: 4

Ingredients:

- 1½ C. fresh mixed berries (raspberries, blueberries, strawberries), chopped
- 2 C. water
- 3 Tbsp unflavored gelatin powder
- 3 Tbsp honey
- 1 tsp lemon zest
- Mint leaves for garnish

Directions:

1. Combine water and honey in a saucepan and bring to a simmer, stir until honey dissolves
2. Sprinkle gelatin powder over the simmering water and whisk until completely dissolved
3. Remove from heat and let cool for a few minutes
4. Stir in the chopped berries and lemon zest
5. Pour the mixture into serving cups and refrigerate until set, about 2 hrs
6. Garnish with fresh mint leaves before serving

Tips:

- Alter the types of berries based on seasonal availability for varied flavor profiles
- If preferred, replace honey with agave syrup for a different sweetness

- Ensure gelatin is completely dissolved to avoid lumpy texture

Nutritional Values: Calories: 120, Fat: 0.5g, Carbs: 25g, Protein: 6g, Sugar: 22g, Sodium: 30 mg, Potassium: 90 mg, Cholesterol: 0 mg

MIXED BERRY SORBET SWIRL

Preparation Time: 20 min
Cooking Time: 3 hr (freezing time)
Mode of Cooking: Freezing
Servings: 4
Ingredients:

- 2 C. mixed berries (strawberries, blackberries, blueberries), pureed
- 1 C. water
- ¾ C. granulated sugar substitute (suitable for diabetics and low-fat diets)
- 1 Tbsp fresh lemon juice
- 1 Tbsp chopped fresh basil

Directions:

1. Combine water and granulated sugar substitute in a pan and heat until the sugar dissolves completely, stirring occasionally
2. Remove from heat and cool to room temperature
3. Add the berry puree, fresh lemon juice, and chopped basil to the sugar mixture
4. Stir thoroughly to combine all ingredients
5. Pour the mixture into an ice cream maker and churn according to manufacturer's instructions until it reaches sorbet consistency
6. Transfer to a storage container and freeze until firm, about 3 hr

Tips:

- Experiment with different berry combinations each time to find your perfect mix
- Stir the sorbet every 30 min while freezing if not using an ice cream maker, to prevent ice crystals from forming
- Decorate with additional basil leaves when serving to enhance flavor and presentation

Nutritional Values: Calories: 90, Fat: 0g, Carbs: 23g, Protein: 1g, Sugar: 20g, Sodium: 5 mg, Potassium: 75 mg, Cholesterol: 0 mg

BERRY QUINOA SALAD DELIGHT

Preparation Time: 25 min
Cooking Time: none
Mode of Cooking: No Cooking
Servings: 6
Ingredients:

- 1½ C. quinoa, cooked and cooled
- 1 C. fresh blueberries
- 1 C. fresh raspberries
- ½ C. pomegranate seeds
- ¼ C. fresh mint, finely chopped
- 2 Tbsp flaxseed oil
- 1 Tbsp balsamic vinegar
- Salt and pepper to taste
- ¼ C. toasted almond slivers for topping

Directions:

1. Combine the cooked quinoa, blueberries, raspberries, and pomegranate seeds in a large bowl
2. In a small bowl, whisk together flaxseed oil, balsamic vinegar, salt, and pepper to create the dressing
3. Pour the dressing over the salad and toss gently to coat
4. Sprinkle with fresh mint and toasted almond slivers before serving

Tips:

- Toasting the almond slivers before adding them to the salad enhances their flavor and adds a wonderful crunch
- Use a mild balsamic vinegar to not overpower the sweetness of the berries
- Adjust the amount of flaxseed oil according to your dietary needs

Nutritional Values: Calories: 215, Fat: 8g, Carbs: 32g, Protein: 6g, Sugar: 8g, Sodium: 10 mg, Potassium: 270 mg, Cholesterol: 0 mg

CINNAMON SPICED BAKED APPLES

Preparation Time: 10 min
Cooking Time: 25 min
Mode of Cooking: Baking
Servings: 4
Ingredients:

- 4 large apples, cored and sliced
- 2 Tbsp honey
- 1 tsp ground cinnamon
- ¼ tsp ground nutmeg
- ½ cup apple juice
- 1 Tbsp cornstarch mixed with 2 Tbsp water
- 1 tsp vanilla extract

Directions:

1. Preheat oven to 350°F (175°C)
2. Arrange apple slices in a baking dish
3. In a bowl, combine honey, cinnamon, nutmeg, and vanilla extract
4. Pour mixture over apples
5. Mix apple juice with cornstarch mixture and pour it over the apples
6. Bake in preheated oven for 25 min or until apples are tender

Tips:

- Serve warm with a dollop of low-fat vanilla yogurt if desired
- Avoid adding extra sugars or toppings to keep it digestion-friendly

Nutritional Values: Calories: 150, Fat: 0.5g, Carbs: 40g, Protein: 0.5g, Sugar: 30g, Sodium: 5 mg, Potassium: 194 mg, Cholesterol: 0 mg

PEACH GINGER COMPOTE

Preparation Time: 5 min
Cooking Time: 15 min
Mode of Cooking: Simmering
Servings: 4
Ingredients:

- 4 peaches, peeled and diced
- 2 Tbsp honey
- 1 Tbsp finely grated fresh ginger
- Juice of 1 lemon
- Lemon zest from 1 lemon
- ½ cup water

Directions:

1. Combine peaches, honey, ginger, lemon juice, and lemon zest in a medium saucepan
2. Add water
3. Bring to a simmer over medium heat and cook for 15 min, stirring occasionally, until peaches are soft and the sauce has thickened slightly

Tips:

- Ideal for topping oatmeal or mixed with low-fat cottage cheese for a protein boost
- Ginger aids in digestion, making this not only delicious but also soothing for the stomach

Nutritional Values: Calories: 120, Fat: 0.3g, Carbs: 31g, Protein: 1.5g, Sugar: 28g, Sodium: 1 mg, Potassium: 285 mg, Cholesterol: 0 mg

BALSAMIC HONEY ROASTED PEARS

Preparation Time: 10 min
Cooking Time: 20 min
Mode of Cooking: Roasting
Servings: 4
Ingredients:

- 4 pears, halved and cored
- 1 Tbsp honey
- 2 Tbsp balsamic vinegar
- ¼ tsp ground cinnamon
- Fresh mint for garnish

Directions:

1. Preheat oven to 375°F (190°C)
2. Arrange pear halves cut-side up in a baking dish
3. Drizzle with honey and balsamic vinegar
4. Sprinkle with cinnamon
5. Roast in the preheated oven for 20 min or until pears are tender

Tips:

- Garnish with fresh mint before serving to enhance flavor
- Pair with a scoop of low-fat frozen yogurt for a decadent yet gentle on the digestion dessert

Nutritional Values: Calories: 110, Fat: 0.2g, Carbs: 29g, Protein: 0.6g, Sugar: 20g, Sodium: 2 mg, Potassium: 212 mg, Cholesterol: 0 mg

10.2 LOW-FAT BAKED GOODS

BANANA WALNUT MUFFINS

Preparation Time: 15 min.
Cooking Time: 20 min.
Mode of Cooking: Baking
Servings: 12
Ingredients:

- 1½ C. whole wheat flour
- 1 tsp baking soda
- ½ tsp salt
- ¼ tsp cinnamon
- 3 ripe bananas, mashed
- ⅓ C. honey
- 1 tsp vanilla extract
- 1 egg, beaten
- ¼ C. unsweetened applesauce
- ¼ C. low-fat milk
- ½ C. walnuts, chopped

Directions:

1. Preheat oven to 375°F (190°C)
2. Whisk together flour, baking soda, salt, and cinnamon in a large bowl
3. In another bowl, combine bananas, honey, vanilla, egg, applesauce, and milk ◊ Add wet ingredients to dry ingredients, stirring until just combined ◊ Fold in walnuts ◊ Spoon batter into prepared muffin tins ◊ Bake for 20 min. or until a toothpick inserted in the center comes out clean

Tips:

- Use overripe bananas for extra sweetness and moisture
- For added texture and heart-healthy fats, sprinkle extra chopped walnuts on top before baking

Nutritional Values: Calories: 190, Fat: 5g, Carbs: 34g, Protein: 4g, Sugar: 14g, Sodium: 180 mg, Potassium: 150 mg, Cholesterol: 18 mg

APPLE CINNAMON OAT MUFFINS

Preparation Time: 20 min.
Cooking Time: 25 min.
Mode of Cooking: Baking
Servings: 12
Ingredients:

- 1 C. rolled oats
- 1 C. whole wheat flour
- 1½ tsp baking powder
- ½ tsp baking soda
- ¼ tsp salt
- 1 tsp cinnamon
- 1 C. unsweetened applesauce
- ½ C. low-fat yogurt
- ¼ C. honey
- 1 egg
- 1 tsp vanilla extract
- 1 large apple, peeled and finely chopped

Directions:

1. Preheat oven to 375°F (190°C)
2. Mix oats, flour, baking powder, baking soda, salt, and cinnamon in a large bowl
3. In another bowl, whisk together applesauce, yogurt, honey, egg, and vanilla ◊ Combine wet and dry ingredients until just mixed ◊ Stir in chopped apple ◊ Spoon batter into muffin cups ◊ Bake for 25 min. or until golden brown

Tips:

- Adding a pinch of nutmeg enhances the flavor
- Can substitute pear for apple for a different taste
- Let muffins cool in the pan for easier removal

Nutritional Values: Calories: 135, Fat: 2g, Carbs: 27g, Protein: 4g, Sugar: 10g, Sodium: 105 mg, Potassium: 75 mg, Cholesterol: 16 mg

ZUCCHINI CARROT MUFFINS

Preparation Time: 20 min.
Cooking Time: 23 min.
Mode of Cooking: Baking
Servings: 12
Ingredients:

- 1 C. whole wheat flour
- ½ C. all-purpose flour
- ½ tsp salt
- 2 tsp baking powder
- ½ tsp cinnamon
- ¼ tsp nutmeg
- 1 large egg
- ½ C. unsweetened applesauce
- ¼ C. honey
- ½ tsp vanilla extract
- 1 medium zucchini, grated
- 1 medium carrot, grated
- ¼ C. raisins

Directions:

1. Preheat oven to 375°F (190°C)
2. Combine both flours, salt, baking powder, cinnamon, and nutmeg in a bowl
3. In another bowl, mix egg, applesauce, honey, and vanilla ◊ Stir wet ingredients into dry until well blended ◊ Fold in grated zucchini, carrot, and raisins ◊ Distribute batter into muffin tins ◊ Bake for 23 min. or until a tester comes out clean

Tips:

- Squeeze excess moisture from zucchini and carrot to keep muffins from being too wet
- Add a tablespoon of flaxseed for an omega-3 boost
- Raisins can be soaked in warm water to make them plumper

Nutritional Values: Calories: 128, Fat: 1g, Carbs: 28g, Protein: 3g, Sugar: 11g, Sodium: 98 mg, Potassium: 137 mg, Cholesterol: 16 mg

APPLE CINNAMON SCONES

Preparation Time: 15 min
Cooking Time: 20 min
Mode of Cooking: Baking
Servings: 8
Ingredients:

- 2 cups whole wheat flour
- 1 Tbsp baking powder
- ¼ tsp salt
- 1 tsp ground cinnamon
- ¼ cup cold, unsalted butter, cubed
- ¼ cup applesauce, unsweetened
- 1 large apple, peeled and finely chopped
- ¼ cup fat-free milk
- 1 large egg
- 2 Tbsp honey

Directions:

1. Preheat oven to 375°F (190°C)
2. In a large bowl, whisk together flour, baking powder, salt, and cinnamon
3. Cut in butter until mixture resembles coarse crumbs
4. In a separate bowl, whisk together applesauce, milk, egg, and honey
5. Add wet ingredients to dry ingredients along with chopped apple; stir just until moistened
6. Turn dough onto a floured surface and pat into an 8-inch circle
7. Cut into 8 wedges and place on a baking sheet lined with parchment paper
8. Bake until golden brown, about 20 min

Tips:

- Use cold butter to ensure light, flaky scones
- Brush tops with a bit of milk before baking for a golden finish
- Serve warm for best flavor

Nutritional Values: Calories: 220, Fat: 6g, Carbs: 34g, Protein: 5g, Sugar: 9g, Sodium: 330 mg, Potassium: 102 mg, Cholesterol: 40 mg

LEMON POPPY SEED SCONES

Preparation Time: 15 min
Cooking Time: 15 min
Mode of Cooking: Baking
Servings: 8
Ingredients:

- 2 cups all-purpose flour
- 1 Tbsp baking powder
- ¼ tsp salt
- 1 Tbsp poppy seeds
- ¼ cup cold, unsalted butter, cubed
- 1 Tbsp lemon zest
- ¼ cup fat-free Greek yogurt
- 1 large egg
- ¼ cup honey
- 2 Tbsp fresh lemon juice

Directions:

1. Preheat oven to 400°F (204°C)
2. Combine flour, baking powder, salt, and poppy seeds in a large bowl
3. Blend in butter until mixture looks like coarse crumbs
4. In another bowl, mix yogurt, egg, honey, and lemon juice and zest
5. Add wet ingredients to dry, mix until just combined
6. Place on lightly floured surface and form into a circle about ¾-inch thick
7. Cut into 8 wedges and place on a lined baking tray
8. Bake until edges are golden, about 15 min

Tips:

- Do not overmix the dough to keep scones light and airy
- Glaze with a mixture of lemon juice and confectioners' sugar after cooling for extra zing
- Perfect with a cup of tea

Nutritional Values: Calories: 180, Fat: 5g, Carbs: 30g, Protein: 4g, Sugar: 8g, Sodium: 320 mg, Potassium: 88 mg, Cholesterol: 30 mg

CHEDDAR SCALLION SCONES

Preparation Time: 20 min
Cooking Time: 20 min
Mode of Cooking: Baking
Servings: 8
Ingredients:

- 2 cups all-purpose flour
- 1½ Tbsp baking powder
- ½ tsp salt
- ⅓ cup cold, unsalted butter, cubed
- ½ cup fat-free sharp cheddar cheese, shredded
- 3 Tbsp scallions, chopped
- ½ cup fat-free milk
- 1 large egg

Directions:

1. Preheat oven to 400°F (204°C)
2. Mix flour, baking powder, and salt in a bowl
3. Cut in butter until crumbly
4. Stir in cheddar and scallions
5. In another bowl, beat milk and egg together and then blend into the flour mixture until just moist
6. Turn onto a floured surface, knead gently, and shape into a round disc
7. Cut into 8 wedges, place on a lined baking sheet, brush with a little milk
8. Bake until golden brown, about 20 min

Tips:

- Use sharp cheddar for more intense flavor
- Serve these scones warm for a melt-in-your-mouth experience
- Pair with a light soup for a fulfilling snack

Nutritional Values: Calories: 200, Fat: 9g, Carbs: 25g, Protein: 6g, Sugar: 1g, Sodium: 460 mg, Potassium: 90 mg, Cholesterol: 55 mg

APPLE SPICE BUNDT CAKE

Preparation Time: 20 min
Cooking Time: 45 min
Mode of Cooking: Baking
Servings: 8
Ingredients:

- 1½ cups all-purpose flour

- ¾ cup apple sauce, unsweetened
- 1 cup coconut sugar
- ¼ cup coconut oil, melted
- 1 tsp baking soda
- ½ tsp salt
- 1 tsp cinnamon
- ½ tsp nutmeg
- ¼ tsp cloves
- 2 Tbsp flaxseed meal
- 6 Tbsp water
- 1 tsp vanilla extract
- 1 large apple, peeled and finely chopped
- 1 Tbsp apple cider vinegar

Directions:

1. Preheat oven to 350°F (175°C)
2. Grease a 9-inch bundt pan with a bit of coconut oil
3. Mix flaxseed meal and water in a small bowl and let sit for 5 min to create flax eggs
4. In a large bowl, combine apple sauce, coconut sugar, melted coconut oil, vanilla extract, and apple cider vinegar
5. Add flax eggs to the bowl and mix well
6. In another bowl, whisk together flour, baking soda, salt, cinnamon, nutmeg, and cloves
7. Gradually add the dry ingredients to the wet ingredients, mixing until just combined
8. Fold in chopped apples
9. Pour batter into prepared bundt pan
10. Bake for 45 min or until a toothpick inserted into the center comes out clean

Tips:

- Let cake cool in pan for 10 min before transferring to a wire rack to cool completely
- Dust with a mix of cinnamon and coconut sugar for a sweet finish
- Serve with a dollop of coconut whipped cream for extra indulgence

Nutritional Values: Calories: 280, Fat: 9g, Carbs: 49g, Protein: 3g, Sugar: 27g, Sodium: 320 mg, Potassium: 115 mg, Cholesterol: 0 mg

CARROT AND PINEAPPLE TEA CAKE

Preparation Time: 30 min
Cooking Time: 50 min
Mode of Cooking: Baking
Servings: 10
Ingredients:

- 2 cups whole wheat pastry flour
- 1 tsp cinnamon
- ½ tsp nutmeg
- 1 tsp baking powder
- ½ tsp baking soda
- ¼ tsp salt
- 1 cup crushed pineapple, in its own juice
- 1 cup grated carrots
- ½ cup applesauce, unsweetened
- ½ cup agave nectar
- ¼ cup canola oil
- 2 tsp vanilla extract
- 1 Tbsp white vinegar
- ½ cup walnuts, chopped

Directions:

1. Preheat oven to 350°F (175°C)
2. Grease and flour a 9x5 inch loaf pan
3. In a bowl, mix together flour, cinnamon, nutmeg, baking powder, baking soda, and salt
4. In another large bowl, combine applesauce, crushed pineapple, grated carrots, agave nectar, canola oil, vanilla extract, and white vinegar ⚖ Blend until smooth
5. Gradually stir in dry ingredients to the wet mixture until just combined
6. Fold in chopped walnuts
7. Pour the batter into the prepared pan
8. Bake for about 50 min, or until a toothpick inserted comes out clean

Tips:

- Allow the cake to cool in the pan for 20 min before removing
- This cake pairs wonderfully with a light almond milk glaze or dusted with powdered sugar
- Store in an airtight container to keep moist

Nutritional Values: Calories: 230, Fat: 7g, Carbs: 40g, Protein: 4g, Sugar: 20g, Sodium: 200 mg, Potassium: 180 mg, Cholesterol: 0 mg

LEMON OLIVE OIL CAKE

Preparation Time: 15 min
Cooking Time: 40 min
Mode of Cooking: Baking
Servings: 12
Ingredients:

- 1¾ cups cake flour
- 1 tsp baking powder
- ½ tsp baking soda
- ¼ tsp salt
- 1 cup granulated sugar
- 3 large eggs
- ⅓ cup extra virgin olive oil
- 1 tsp vanilla extract
- 1 Tbsp lemon zest
- ¼ cup lemon juice
- ½ cup almond milk, unsweetened
- Powdered sugar for dusting

Directions:

1. Prelift oven to 350°F (175°C)
2. Grease and flour a 9-inch round cake pan
3. In a bowl, whisk together cake flour, baking powder, baking soda, and salt
4. In another bowl, beat together eggs and sugar until light and fluffy
5. Gradually beat in olive oil, vanilla extract, lemon zest, and lemon juice until well combined
6. Alternate adding dry ingredients and almond milk to the egg mixture, starting and ending with dry ingredients
7. Pour batter into prepared pan
8. Bake for 40 min or until a toothpick inserted in the center comes out clean

Tips:

- Let cake cool in the pan for 10 min, then remove to a wire rack to cool completely
- Dust with powdered sugar before serving

- Excellent with a cup of herbal tea or a scoop of non-dairy ice cream

Nutritional Values: Calories: 210, Fat: 9g, Carbs: 29g, Protein: 4g, Sugar: 17g, Sodium: 150 mg, Potassium: 39 mg, Cholesterol: 55 mg

10.3 GUILT-FREE SWEET TREATS

CHIA AND RASPBERRY PUDDING

Preparation Time: 15 min
Cooking Time: none
Mode of Cooking: No Cooking
Servings: 4
Ingredients:

- 1 C. unsweetened almond milk
- ⅓ C. chia seeds
- 1 cup fresh raspberries
- 2 Tbsp honey or agave syrup (optional)
- ½ tsp vanilla extract
- Fresh mint leaves for garnishing

Directions:

1. Combine almond milk, chia seeds, and vanilla extract in a bowl and stir well
2. Let the mixture sit for about 10 min until the chia seeds swell
3. Add fresh raspberries and gently fold into the mixture
4. Refrigerate for at least 4 hr or overnight until set

Tips:

- Serve chilled topped with mint leaves for a refreshing twist
- If more sweetness is desired, drizzle with a little honey or agave syrup before serving

Nutritional Values: Calories: 130, Fat: 6g, Carbs: 15g, Protein: 4g, Sugar: 7g, Sodium: 30 mg, Potassium: 200 mg, Cholesterol: 0 mg

AVOCADO LIME SORBET

Preparation Time: 20 min
Cooking Time: none
Mode of Cooking: Freezing
Servings: 6

Ingredients:

- 2 ripe avocados, peeled and pitted
- Juice of 2 limes
- ¼ C. erythritol or stevia
- 1 tsp lime zest
- 2 C. cold water
- Fresh lime slices for garnish

Directions:

1. Blend avocados, lime juice, lime zest, and erythritol or stevia in a food processor until smooth
2. Gradually add water and continue blending until incorporated
3. Pour mixture into a freezer-safe container and freeze for at least 5 hr, stirring every hour to break up ice crystals

Tips:

- Serve garnished with lime slices for added zing
- For smoother texture, let sorbet sit at room temperature for 10 min before serving

Nutritional Values: Calories: 120, Fat: 9g, Carbs: 10g, Protein: 2g, Sugar: 1g, Sodium: 5 mg, Potassium: 290 mg, Cholesterol: 0 mg

COCONUT FLOUR LEMON BARS

Preparation Time: 15 min
Cooking Time: 20 min
Mode of Cooking: Baking
Servings: 8
Ingredients:

- For the crust: 1 C. coconut flour
- ⅓ C. coconut oil, melted
- 2 Tbsp erythritol or stevia
- For the filling: Juice and zest of 3 lemons
- 4 eggs
- ½ C. erythritol or stevia
- ¼ C. unsweetened almond milk

Directions:

1. Preheat oven to 350°F (175°C)
2. Combine coconut flour, melted coconut oil, and erythritol in a bowl and press into the bottom of a greased 8x8 inch baking dish
3. Bake for 10 min

4. Whisk together lemon juice, lemon zest, eggs, erythritol, and almond milk and pour over the baked crust
5. Return to oven and bake for an additional 10 min or until set

Tips:

- Allow to cool before slicing
- Serve chilled for a firmer texture
- Garnish with a sprinkle of lemon zest for a citrusy flair

Nutritional Values: Calories: 140, Fat: 10g, Carbs: 12g, Protein: 4g, Sugar: 1g, Sodium: 70 mg, Potassium: 50 mg, Cholesterol: 90 mg

CHIA LEMON DRIZZLE CAKE

Preparation Time: 15 min
Cooking Time: 30 min
Mode of Cooking: Baking
Servings: 8
Ingredients:

- 1½ cups all-purpose flour
- 1 tsp baking powder
- ½ tsp baking soda
- ¼ tsp salt
- ½ cup granulated sugar
- 1 Tbsp lemon zest
- ¼ cup lemon juice
- ½ cup unsweetened applesauce
- ¼ cup low-fat yogurt
- 3 Tbsp chia seeds
- 2 Tbsp olive oil
- ¼ cup almond milk

Directions:

1. Preheat oven to 350°F (175°C)
2. In a bowl, mix flour, baking powder, baking soda, and salt
3. In another bowl, combine sugar, lemon zest, lemon juice, applesauce, yogurt, olive oil, and almond milk
4. Gradually mix dry ingredients into wet until smooth
5. Fold in chia seeds
6. Pour batter into a greased loaf pan

7. Bake for 30 min or until a toothpick inserted in the center comes out clean

Tips:
- Store in an airtight container to keep moist
- Serve with a dollop of low-fat Greek yogurt for added flavor

Nutritional Values: Calories: 180, Fat: 4g, Carbs: 32g, Protein: 4g, Sugar: 12g, Sodium: 210mg, Potassium: 90mg, Cholesterol: 0mg

MINI PEAR AND CINNAMON CRISPS

Preparation Time: 20 min
Cooking Time: 15 min
Mode of Cooking: Baking
Servings: 6
Ingredients:
- 2 large pears, thinly sliced
- 1 tsp ground cinnamon
- 1 Tbsp honey
- ½ cup rolled oats
- ¼ cup whole wheat flour
- 1 Tbsp brown sugar
- 2 Tbsp coconut oil, melted

Directions:
1. Preheat oven to 375°F (190°C)
2. Arrange pear slices on a baking sheet
3. In a small bowl, mix honey and cinnamon, brush over pears
4. Combine oats, flour, brown sugar, and melted coconut oil until crumbly
5. Sprinkle crumble mixture over pears
6. Bake for 15 min or until topping is golden

Tips:
- Enjoy warm or store in an airtight container for up to 2 days
- Perfect topping for low-fat vanilla ice cream or Greek yogurt

Nutritional Values: Calories: 110, Fat: 4g, Carbs: 18g, Protein: 2g, Sugar: 10g, Sodium: 5mg, Potassium: 120mg, Cholesterol: 0mg

GINGER MANGO MOUSSE

Preparation Time: 10 min
Cooking Time: none
Mode of Cooking: No Cooking
Servings: 4
Ingredients:
- 1 large ripe mango, peeled and cubed
- 1 cup silken tofu
- 1½ Tbsp ginger, freshly grated
- 2 Tbsp honey
- 1 tsp lime zest
- Mint leaves for garnish

Directions:
1. Blend mango, silken tofu, ginger, honey, and lime zest until smooth
2. Divide the mixture among dessert glasses
3. Chill in the refrigerator for at least 2 hrs before serving
4. Garnish with mint leaves before serving

Tips:
- Can be made ahead and stored in the refrigerator overnight
- Serve chilled to enhance the flavors

Nutritional Values: Calories: 120, Fat: 1.5g, Carbs: 25g, Protein: 3g, Sugar: 20g, Sodium: 10mg, Potassium: 200mg, Cholesterol: 0mg

CHERRY CHIA PUDDING DELIGHT

Preparation Time: 15 min
Cooking Time: none
Mode of Cooking: No Cooking
Servings: 4
Ingredients:
- 2 C. almond milk, unsweetened
- ½ C. chia seeds
- 1 C. cherries, pitted and chopped
- 1 tsp vanilla extract
- 2 Tbsp honey
- Mint leaves, for garnish

Directions:
1. Combine almond milk and chia seeds in a bowl, mix thoroughly

2. Add chopped cherries, vanilla extract, and honey, mix again until well combined
3. Refrigerate for at least 4 hours or overnight to set
4. Serve chilled, garnished with mint leaves

Tips:

- Can be served with a dollop of fat-free Greek yogurt for added protein
- Customize with different berries for variety in flavors and nutrients

Nutritional Values: Calories: 180, Fat: 8g, Carbs: 23g, Protein: 5g, Sugar: 12g, Sodium: 30 mg, Potassium: 150 mg, Cholesterol: 0 mg

SPICED ROASTED PEAR CUPS

Preparation Time: 10 min
Cooking Time: 25 min
Mode of Cooking: Baking
Servings: 6
Ingredients:

- 3 large pears, halved and cored
- 1 Tbsp honey
- 1 tsp cinnamon
- ¼ tsp nutmeg
- ½ C. crushed walnuts
- ¼ C. rolled oats
- 1 Tbsp coconut oil, melted

Directions:

1. Preheat oven to 375°F (190°C)
2. Arrange pear halves on a baking tray
3. In a bowl, mix together honey, cinnamon, nutmeg, crushed walnuts, rolled oats, and melted coconut oil
4. Spoon the mixture into the center of each pear half
5. Bake for 25 min or until pears are tender

Tips:

- Pears can be served warm or cold
- Pair with a scoop of sugar-free vanilla ice cream for an extra treat
- Excellent source of fiber and natural sweetness

Nutritional Values: Calories: 150, Fat: 8g, Carbs: 22g, Protein: 3g, Sugar: 15g, Sodium: 2 mg, Potassium: 200 mg, Cholesterol: 0 mg

AVOCADO COCOA MOUSSE

Preparation Time: 10 min
Cooking Time: none
Mode of Cooking: Mixing
Servings: 4
Ingredients:

- 2 ripe avocados, peeled and pitted
- ¼ C. cocoa powder, unsweetened
- ¼ C. almond milk, unsweetened
- 3 Tbsp maple syrup
- 1 tsp vanilla extract
- Pinch of salt

Directions:

1. Combine all ingredients in a food processor
2. Blend until smooth and creamy
3. Chill in the refrigerator for at least 1 hour before serving

Tips:

- Sweeten further with stevia if a sweeter taste is desired
- Garnish with a sprinkle of grated dark chocolate for a rich flavor profile
- Avocado provides healthy fats that are essential for no-gallbladder diets

Nutritional Values: Calories: 200, Fat: 15g, Carbs: 20g, Protein: 3g, Sugar: 10g, Sodium: 30 mg, Potassium: 487 mg, Cholesterol: 0 mg

CHAPTER 11: 4-WEEK MEAL PLAN

Embarking on a new dietary journey after your gallbladder surgery can feel like navigating uncharted waters. The prospect of adjusting your meals might seem daunting, yet with the right guide, you'll discover that this new route is not just manageable, but also enjoyable. Over the next four weeks, you'll embark on a structured, yet flexible meal plan designed to introduce you to a diverse range of dishes that cater specifically to your modified dietary needs, ensuring each meal is as delicious as it is digestible.

Imagine this: by the end of the first week, you've already mastered the basics of what foods work best for your body. You start to feel more confident in your choices, understanding that discomfort after eating isn't something you have to live with. As you move into the second week, you'll begin to routine these choices, finding ease and perhaps even pleasure in the preparation and consumption of meals that fuel your body without causing distress.

The third week ushers in an exciting phase of exploration. It's time to broaden your culinary horizon, introducing new ingredients that perhaps you've not dared to try before. This is when your kitchen becomes a place of discovery and your meals transform into a source of joy rather than a cause of anxiety.

By the fourth week, you'll have not just adjusted but embraced this new way of eating. You've learned that living without a gallbladder doesn't mean living without flavor or enjoyment of food. Instead, you are mastering a diet that's as rich in variety as it is in nutrients—custom-designed for your specific health needs.

This chapter is not just a meal plan; it's a roadmap towards regaining confidence in your dietary choices and joy in your meals. Each recipe has been crafted to ensure compatibility with your digestive needs, while also keeping the flavors delightful and preparation straightforward. Let's journey together through these four transformative weeks, discovering that every meal can indeed be an enjoyable experience.

11.1 WEEK 1: STARTING SMOOTHLY

WEEK 1	breakfast	snack	lunch	snack	dinner
Monday	Tropical Mango and Turmeric Smoothie	Crisp Rainbow Pepper Cups	Kale and Apple Salad with Lemon Dressing	Roasted Red Pepper Hummus	Ginger-Soy Poached Cod
Tuesday	Green Apple and Spinach Detox Shake	Avocado Cucumber Rolls	Spinach Quinoa Salad with Pomegranate Seeds	Beetroot Walnut Dip	Lemon-Thyme Baked Tilapia
Wednesday	Berry Beetroot Blast Smoothie	Herbed Jicama Sticks	Beet and Carrot Slaw with Citrus Vinaigrette	Carrot Ginger Spread	Chili Lime Shrimp Skewers
Thursday	Vanilla Almond Protein Smoothie	Pear and Raspberry Crisp	Tarragon Chicken Salad with Grapes	White Bean and Rosemary Spread	Herbed Turkey Breast with Orange Zest
Friday	Berry Blast Protein Shake	Apple Chia Pudding	Lemon Herb Quinoa & Chickpea Salad	Curried Lentil Hummus	Baked Lemon and Dill Chicken
Saturday	Peanut Butter Banana Protein Smoothie	Banana Blueberry Bars	Asian Tofu and Edamame Salad	Herbed Chickpea and Yogurt Dip	Pan-Seared Cod with Parsley Gremolata
Sunday	Berry Beet Morning Bliss	Vanilla Cinnamon Yogurt Delight	Curried Turkey and Avocado Wrap with Whole Wheat Tortilla	Cucumber Yogurt Dip	Quinoa and Black Bean Stuffed Peppers

11.2 WEEK 2: BUILDING ROUTINE

WEEK 2	breakfast	snack	lunch	snack	dinner
Monday	Scrambled Tofu with Spinach	Berry Bliss Yogurt Parfait	Smoked Salmon and Cucumber Wholegrain Bagel	Golden Beet and Fennel Soup	Cauliflower Tofu Tikka Masala
Tuesday	Poached Eggs over Asparagus	Peanut Butter Banana Yogurt	Chickpea Hummus and Veggie Lavash Wrap	Carrot Ginger Soup Cups	Quinoa Tabbouleh with Lemon Mint Dressing
Wednesday	Mushroom and Herb Frittata	Zesty Chickpea Salad Cups	Turkey Avocado Wrap	Chilled Cucumber Avocado Soup	Millet Risotto with Roasted Butternut Squash
Thursday	Zucchini and Tomato Basil Omelette	Mini Polenta Cakes with Sun-Dried Tomato Tapenade	Grilled Chicken Hummus Wrap	Herby Yogurt Avocado Dip	Barley and Kale Pilaf with Walnuts
Friday	Bell Pepper and Onion Mini Quiches	Avocado and White Bean Wrap Bites	Beef and Mustard Greens Wrap	Roasted Red Pepper and Yogurt Hummus	Tomato Basil Coulis
Saturday	Cauliflower and Kale Egg Muffins	Cucumber Ribbon Salad with Apple Cider Vinaigrette	Mediterranean Hummus Veggie Wrap	Cucumber Yogurt Dip	Zesty Ginger Carrot Sauce
Sunday	Herbed Mushroom and Spinach Frittata	Beet and Carrot Slaw with Citrus Honey Dressing	Carrot and Avocado California Wrap	Curried Lentil Hummus	Avocado Cilantro Lime Dressing

11.3 WEEK 3: EXPANDING VARIETY

WEEK 3	breakfast	snack	lunch	snack	dinner
Monday	Quinoa Apple Cinnamon Porridge	Apple Spice Bundt Cake	Ginger Turmeric Chicken Broth	Berry Quinoa Salad Delight	Smoked Salmon and Dill Scramble
Tuesday	Millet Pumpkin Porridge	Carrot and Pineapple Tea Cake	Fennel and Leek Vegetable Broth	Cinnamon Spiced Baked Apples	Tomato Basil Omelette
Wednesday	Buckwheat and Berry Porridge	Lemon Olive Oil Cake	Miso Mushroom Broth	Peach Ginger Compote	Beet and Carrot Slaw with Citrus Vinaigrette
Thursday	Cinnamon Pear Barley Porridge	Chia and Raspberry Pudding	Silken Tofu and Mushroom Soup	Balsamic Honey Roasted Pears	Asian Tofu and Edamame Salad
Friday	Savory Quinoa and Vegetable Porridge	Avocado Lime Sorbet	Cauliflower Leek Soup with Nutritional Yeast	Mini Pear and Cinnamon Crisps	Chicken and Broccoli Casserole with Brown Rice Pasta
Saturday	Apple Cinnamon Buckwheat Hot Cereal	Coconut Flour Lemon Bars	Carrot Ginger Soup with Apple	Ginger Mango Mousse	Spring Green Risotto
Sunday	Cinnamon Walnut Oatmeal	Chia Lemon Drizzle Cake	Turkey and Vegetable Medley Soup	Cherry Chia Pudding Delight	Spiced Sweet Potato and Red Onion Saute

11.4 WEEK 4: MASTERING THE DIET

WEEK 4	breakfast	snack	lunch	snack	dinner
Monday	Pumpkin Seed Chia Porridge	Vanilla Cinnamon Yogurt Delight	Beef and Mustard Greens Wrap	Golden Beet and Fennel Soup	Herbed Turkey Breast with Orange Zest
Tuesday	Almond Spice Millet Bowl	Berry Bliss Yogurt Parfait	Mediterranean Hummus Veggie Wrap	Carrot Ginger Soup Cups	Baked Lemon and Dill Chicken
Wednesday	Scrambled Tofu with Spinach	Peanut Butter Banana Yogurt	Carrot and Avocado California Wrap	Chilled Cucumber Avocado Soup	Pan-Seared Cod with Parsley Gremolata
Thursday	Poached Eggs over Asparagus	Zesty Chickpea Salad Cups	Spicy Tofu Lettuce Wrap	Herby Yogurt Avocado Dip	Quinoa and Black Bean Stuffed Peppers
Friday	Mushroom and Herb Frittata	Mini Polenta Cakes with Sun-Dried Tomato Tapenade	Ginger Turmeric Chicken Broth	Roasted Red Pepper and Yogurt Hummus	Cauliflower Tofu Tikka Masala
Saturday	Zucchini and Tomato Basil Omelette	Avocado and White Bean Wrap Bites	Fennel and Leek Vegetable Broth	Cucumber Yogurt Dip	Quinoa Tabbouleh with Lemon Mint Dressing
Sunday	Bell Pepper and Onion Mini Quiches	Cucumber Ribbon Salad with Apple Cider Vinaigrette	Miso Mushroom Broth	Curried Lentil Hummus	Millet Risotto with Roasted Butternut Squash

DOWNLOAD YOUR BONUSES

BONUS 1 - 30 Unique Mediterranean Diet Recipes

BONUS 2 – Eating out after gallbladder removal

BONUS 3 – Balancing Health and flavour

Thank you so much for purchasing my Cookbook and downloading the bonus!

I'm truly grateful for your support and hope the recipes and tips help make your post-surgery journey a little easier and more enjoyable. Your feedback means the world to me, and I'd love to hear what you think.

If you have a moment, please consider leaving a review on Amazon—your thoughts will not only help me improve but also guide others looking for the right resources.

Wishing you all the best on this journey!

CHAPTER 12: RESOURCES AND SUPPORT

As we draw near the end of our journey together through "The Practical No Gallbladder Diet Cookbook," I hope the recipes and tips shared have brought both confidence and delight back into your meals. Yet, the path to mastering your post-gallbladder removal diet does not end here; it is an ongoing process of learning, adapting, and discovering. To further support and enhance your dietary adventure, this final chapter is dedicated to providing you with an array of additional resources and networks that aim to support you every step of the way. Navigating your new diet can sometimes feel like sailing in uncharted waters. Where do you turn when you encounter a rare ingredient? What do you do when a sudden dietary question pops up at a family dinner or during a late night? It's crucial to have a beacon or a compass in the form of reliable resources and a supportive community.

In your day-to-day life, where meal planning might feel like a solitary task, remember that you are part of a broader community—a network of individuals who understand the nuances and necessities of living well without a gallbladder. From glossaries that demystify complex nutritional terms to FAQs that address common and not-so-common queries, this chapter aims to equip you with tools to find answers and encouragement swiftly and reliably.

Furthermore, the inclusion of support networks emphasizes that you are never alone in this. These communities, both online and perhaps local to you, can offer personal insights and encouragement that transform challenges into shared experiences and victories. Engaging with others who are navigating similar dietary paths can not only provide emotional solace but also practical advice that might not be found in any guidebook.

So, as you continue to adapt and enjoy your gallbladder-free diet, let this chapter serve as your guide to the wealth of information and community support available. Embrace the resources provided with the same enthusiasm with which you have embarked on making every meal enjoyable and nourishing. Here's to continued exploration and joy in your culinary adventures!

12.1 GLOSSARY OF INGREDIENTS AND TERMS

In our culinary journey post-gallbladder removal, you've encountered many ingredients, some familiar and others perhaps esoteric and curious. Within these pages, we've touched upon a cornucopia of foods, each with their specific benefits or restrictions, uniquely tailored to meet the needs of a no-gallbladder diet. From almond milk to zucchini, your diet has been redefined with an eye toward gentleness and digestibility. Here, we delve into not just the "what" of these ingredients and terms but also the "why" and "how" they function in your diet, shedding light on their significance in your daily fare.

Let's start with the basics: **fats**. Gone are the days when all fats were seen as culprits. Now, we differentiate. **Monounsaturated** and **polyunsaturated fats**, found in avocados and fish, respectively, are champions in our meals, offering both digestibility and nutritious benefits without overwhelming a gallbladder-free system. On the flip side, **saturated fats** and, worse, **trans fats**—often lurking in processed foods and baked goods—demand caution and moderation.

In our discussions about protein, we've balanced the scales between animal and plant sources. The term **lean protein** is not just dietary jargon but a crucial guideline. Think chicken breast over thighs, beans over beef. These choices aren't arbitrary. Lean proteins provide the necessary nutrients without excessive fats, making digestion smoother and symptoms less likely.

And let's not forget **fiber**—a term that pops up in every health dialogue, yet often misunderstood. Soluble fiber, such as that in apples and oats, becomes gel-like in the stomach, aiding in gentle digestion, while **insolubility**

fiber, from carrots and whole grains, helps to keep things moving rhythmically, reducing the risk of uncomfortable bloating or constipation.

Navigating this glossary, consider **phenols** and **tannins**, often overshadowed yet significant. Found in many teas and some fruits, these can affect digestion and should be approached with knowledge and moderation. Transitioning into more specific terms, **gluten**—a protein that has become a household word, brings about concern not only to those with celiac disease but also for individuals sensitive to inflammatory foods post-surgery.

Another pivotal term is **glycemic index**, a number assigned to food based on how slowly or quickly it causes increases in blood glucose levels. Foods low on this index are pivotal in a no-gallbladder diet, providing gradual energy release and minimizing digestive stress.

On the more technical side, **emulsifiers** might sound like a food industry term, but understanding these can help you choose better food products. These agents help in blending ingredients like oil and water which naturally separate. On food labels, common emulsifiers include lecithin and guar gum, often necessary in low-fat products but should be consumed in moderation.

As we've recommended smaller portion sizes, the term **low-density food** has also been crucial. These foods fill you up with fewer calories, usually high in fiber, water, and nutrients, perfect for managing a healthy weight and reducing the workload on your digestive system.

Herbs and spices, like **turmeric** and **ginger**, have been highlighted not just for their ability to enhance flavor but for their anti-inflammatory properties, which are beneficial in managing gastrointestinal discomfort. Similarly, **probiotics** found in yogurt and fermented foods have been noted for their role in maintaining gut health, an essential post-cholecystectomy consideration.

Throughout this guide, we've also discussed **enzyme supplementation** as a means to aid digestion. Terms like **pancreatic lipase**, an enzyme aiding in fat digestion, provide a window into understanding why certain supplements might be necessary to support your body's adjusted digestive capabilities.

In transitioning your lifestyle, knowledge of these terms and ingredients not only enriches your understanding but empowers your day-to-day choices. Each term, ingredient, and nutritional strategy discussed isn't just academic; they're practical parts of living well without a gallbladder. This glossary equips you with the knowledge to decode labels, understand dietary advice, and choose foods that celebrate and support your body's new way of living.

As we continue moving forward, let this chapter be a reference to keep coming back to—a source of clarity and empowerment on your dietary journey. Each term here is a stepping stone to a balanced, healthful lifestyle that embraces the full joy of eating without discomfort or fear.

12.2 FREQUENTLY ASKED QUESTIONS

Navigating life after gallbladder surgery comes with a myriad of questions. From understanding what foods to eat to managing discomfort, it's essential to have reliable and accurate answers that guide and reassure you. Over the course of this book, various questions have arisen, echoed by many who have embarked on this journey. Here, consolidated for your ease and learning, are answers to some of the most frequently asked questions by individuals sharing your experience.

What foods should I strictly avoid post-gallbladder removal? The answer isn't always straightforward as individual tolerance can vary. However, typically, high-fat foods, very spicy foods, and sometimes dairy products are known to cause difficulties. These foods can overstimulate the liver's bile production, which, without the regulatory function of the gallbladder, might lead to discomfort and digestive issues. Instead, a focus on lean proteins, whole grains, and plenty of fruits and vegetables is recommended.

Why do I need to eat smaller meals throughout the day? Without your gallbladder to store and concentrate bile, bile flows into your intestine more continuously but in smaller amounts. Larger meals require more bile for digestion, so when you eat a big meal, there might not be enough bile available to properly break down large amounts of fat at one time. Smaller, more frequent meals can help manage this by matching the availability of bile with the demand for digestion.

What if I still experience symptoms even after adjusting my diet? This can happen, and it's important to consult with your healthcare provider. They might suggest further dietary adjustments, medications to bind bile acid, or even supplements to aid digestion. Remember, finding the right dietary balance can take time, and individual responses can vary significantly.

Can I ever eat normally again? "Normally" might take on a new definition. Many individuals find that they can gradually reintroduce various foods as their body adjusts to the absence of the gallbladder. The key is gradual reintroduction and careful monitoring of how your body reacts. It's also important to continue to eat smaller portions and perhaps avoid very high-fat meals to prevent discomfort.

Are there long-term effects of not having a gallbladder? For most people, the answer is no. The body is adaptable, and while the initial adjustments can be challenging, most individuals find a new normal. However, staying informed, monitoring how different foods affect you, and continuing to follow a balanced diet are essential steps to ensure you remain symptom-free.

How do I handle social situations like dining out? Planning ahead is crucial. You can look up restaurant menus in advance to identify meals that are suitable for your diet. Don't hesitate to ask for dishes to be prepared without specific ingredients that cause you issues. Most restaurants are accommodating when they're given clear instructions. Additionally, eating a small snack before you go out can ensure that you're not overly hungry and prone to making rapid food choices that may not suit your digestion.

Is it necessary to take supplements post-surgery? This depends on individual needs and dietary adjustments. Some might benefit from bile acid binders or digestive enzymes, and others might require vitamin supplements, particularly if they're struggling with malabsorption. A detailed discussion with your healthcare provider can determine if supplements are necessary and which ones would benefit your health.

Will I need to be on a special diet forever? Post-gallbladder removal, the diet isn't about restriction but about understanding and responding to your new digestive system's needs. Many find that once they adjust, many foods can be reintroduced, and they can eat a varied and balanced diet. The diet becomes not so much about limiting life but enriching it with choices that feel good.

What happens if I ignore dietary advice? Ignoring dietary guidelines can lead to discomfort, like bloating, gas, and diarrhea, and sometimes more severe issues such as bile acid diarrhea or fat malabsorption. Following the advice not only helps in avoiding discomfort but also in promoting long-term health.

How can I ensure I'm getting balanced nutrition? Balancing nutrition involves eating a wide variety of foods within the guidelines suggested, ensuring you get a good mix of macronutrients and micronutrients. Regular check-ups with a nutritionist or healthcare provider can also help monitor and adjust your diet to ensure your body is getting what it needs.

Living without a gallbladder certainly requires adjustments, but with informed choices and mindful eating, it's not just manageable; it can be a pathway to an even healthier lifestyle. Each question and answer, while providing a guideline, also encourages personal exploration and adaptation, reflecting the unique way your body responds to life post-gallbladder removal.

12.3 Additional Resources and Support Networks

In navigating the waters of post-gallbladder removal, the sea may sometimes seem vast and a little daunting. Amidst managing your diet and adapting to new lifestyle changes, having a supportive community and reliable resources can be likened to finding safe harbors in the midst of a storm. This sub-chapter is dedicated to directing you towards various beacons of support, educational platforms, and communities that resonate with your journey towards a healthy post-surgical life.

The value of a well-informed support network cannot be overstated. Imagine, for a moment, a network that extends beyond the pages of this book—a bustling community where stories are shared, advice is given, and comfort received. These networks, whether online forums, local support groups, or medical professionals specializing in post-gallbladder removal care, are invaluable.

Online Forums and Social Media Groups: Platforms such as Reddit, Facebook, and specific health forums offer communities where individuals share personal experiences, dietary tips, and emotional support. Engaging in these groups can help you feel less isolated as you adjust to your new normal. They provide a platform to both receive and offer advice based on real-life experiences, ranging from managing diet to finding the right medical care.

Healthcare Providers: Building a strong relationship with your healthcare provider—be it a gastroenterologist, a dietitian, or your primary care provider—is crucial. They are not only your primary source of medical advice but also your guide in the intricacies of health management post-surgery. Don't hesitate to reach out to them with your concerns or for referrals to specialists like registered dietitians who can offer tailored advice and monitor your health progress.

Educative Websites and Health Blogs: Websites such as Mayo Clinic, WebMD, and specific digestive health sites provide scientifically backed information that can help you understand your condition and learn how to manage it better. These resources often have articles written by medical professionals and digestible summaries of the latest research.

Cookbooks and Nutritional Guides: While this book provides a detailed guide to eating well without a gallbladder, exploring other cookbooks that focus on low-fat, healthy eating can offer new recipes and inspire you to broaden your dietary options. Look for books and guides that are vetted by nutritionists and align with the dietary advice relevant to gallbladder health.

Local Support Groups: Depending on your location, there may be local support groups that meet regularly, providing a space to connect with others facing similar challenges. These groups can offer a sense of community and real-time support that online forums may not fully replicate. Hospitals or community centers often have information on such groups.

Professional Counseling: Adjusting to life post-surgery can also be challenging emotionally and mentally. Professional counselors or therapists, especially those who specialize in chronic illness or health-related life changes, can provide tools to manage stress, anxiety, or depression that might arise from your health issues.

Nutritional Counseling: Registered dietitians (RDs) or nutritionists specializing in digestive health can be pivotal in your journey. They can help develop meal plans, suggest dietary adjustments, and provide detailed strategies to manage symptoms through diet.

Continuing Medical Education: For those who want to dive deeper into understanding their condition, many hospitals and educational institutions offer lectures, workshops, and seminars on digestive health and nutrition. These can provide advanced knowledge and the latest updates in medical care.

Apps and Trackers: Numerous health apps are available that can help you monitor your diet, track symptoms, and even connect you with nutritionists or doctors. Utilizing these tools can help you maintain an effective diet and quickly identify foods or activities that exacerbate symptoms.

Engaging with these resources and networks allows for a holistic approach to managing your health post-gallbladder removal. Each resource serves as a tool, a guide, and sometimes a companion on your journey to wellness. By tapping into these support systems, you're not just surviving; you're thriving, armed with knowledge and a community that understands and supports your path to recovery and health.